Praise for
A Second Chance at Dancing

~

"Part fiction, part memoir, *A Second Chance at Dancing* re-counts a soul-searching quest reminiscent of the great 20th-century existentialist narratives, intensely personal but striking deep roots into the human condition. Tusa gives us not a string of events but a site of reflection, a circling down, as his narrator slowly opens a hidden emotional landscape. When the plot hits, it hits powerfully, but the real story remains the inner story.

"In some sense, the narrator, Michael, is everyman, too old for coming-of-age, too young for a mid-life crisis. He is a bit like Camus's Meursault but laden with emotional content, a bit like Salinger's Holden but more mature. With analytical precision – and an eye on the emotional limits of that analytical precision – he grapples with his budding career, with the siren call of the barroom, and with the meaning of life. And of relationships. But especially one relationship. Caroline. Caroline is pure and enigmatic, but sensual and present. One gets the sense that she too is just a human being, but that she alone can wedge something open in the narrator, something that gives him – and us – an ephemeral glimpse at something universal and very solemn about the human experience."

—Gary Gautier, Ph.D., author of *Hippies, Mr. Robert's Bones*, and *Year of the Butterfly*

A Second Chance at Dancing

A Second Chance at Dancing

A MEMOIR OF SORTS

Michael T. Tusa Jr.

Red High Top Press

Red High Top Press
Abita Springs, LA

redhightoppress.com

Printed and manufactured in the United States of America

ISBN: 978-1-7321933-0-7

Library of Congress Control Number: 2018904579

Book design by Cherry Press

In Memory of Caroline Gandy

A Memoir of Sorts: Memoirs are supposed to be 100% factually accurate. This one is not. It was, however, inspired by actual events in my life. Names are changed in some places, time periods shifted and a character or two was inserted for narrative purposes.

A Second Chance at Dancing

ONE

~

I f you must know, I really didn't feel like talking about it at first. How to describe "it" to others? What name to give to a confluence of lost memories, of childhood abuses and the unrecognized value of love and friendship? Words, I have learned, sometimes snare you in a straightjacket of unintended meaning. I didn't want to be misunderstood. Throughout my life I had used language, often as a shield, as part of a well developed resistance to social norms, and also to conceal my emotions. I had never attained much of an understanding of emotions, or more accurately, of my dearth of emotional responses. It was an unexplored and often impenetrable region of my psyche with childhood locks which I could not open. Besides, I had to solve my past before I could understand the present, contemplate the future, or tell our story. And ultimately it was our story, Caroline's and mine.

It was a time in my life when I was trying to discern what was happening to me, what long burning flames had been suddenly extinguished and which illusions about myself were finally being laid bare. In all candor, most of my energy in those early days, the traumatic aftermath, was spent trying to retain my grasp on the hard reality of the simple day-to-day tasks that made up the unthinking, self-immolating momentum of my life. I had a tendency to drift off mentally into imaginary landscapes, where the fall leaves of Maine mixed with the familiarity of a New Orleans neighborhood bar and provided me with an armored protection against a new and unfamiliar pain.

I began having vivid dreams, the details of which I could recall upon waking and which remained fresh with me for days afterwards. Dreams in which the spirits and the supernatural were reduced to the common. Repeated dreams where I had no home, no place to live, and tired and beaten, was turned away each time at the door of my childhood home by my father. I would wake from such dreams in physical discomfort. It was hard to tell what Jungian symbolic messages, if any, such dreams contained. I spent days alternatively consoled and frustrated by those dreams, trying to decide which to hold onto, rely upon and unravel, and which to simply discard.

I also did not initially talk much about it because I did not think it was anyone else's business how the two of us had lived our lives, the numinous tension between my constant rebellion and Caroline's revelation, and what had been important to us. I resented any attempt by others to reduce what they did not understand to a common, but meaningless, language, to the limits of their own experience. I wanted to strip my life naked to its essentials, to the cemetery of my intellect, to remove its absurd elements, and examine these quietly by myself. Once that process was far enough along, and my balance was returning, I guess I thought I would be ready and not be weighed down by self-identity's grip, or the all too frail human need to build and embellish memories. Besides, I was also having trouble remembering certain things that I had done, or that had occurred between us, things sitting on the hem of my consciousness. I knew from my childhood that I had a tremendous ability to forget. It was actually not forgetting, but blocking things out, restricting my own vision with a false solemnity, to protect some still vital part of me. At least I know that now.

After several months, however, I began treating it like a long anticipated game of chess and preferred to make my move first by talking about it, before the insincere questioning from others began. My analytical abilities, which had developed as inner armament, predisposed me, I suppose, to dealing with it in such a manner. In those days I tended to see the world only through the lens of my intellect. Now, with the passage of time, it's somewhat easier, especially since my memory of events has started to improve. When I can, I usually try to start at the beginning. Even though it's repetitive, it helps me when I repeat the sequence of events.

Marxist theory. My research has focused, however, on Mikhail Bakunin, an anarchist who was a contemporary of Marx. I am hopeful of doing a paper on Bakunin's critique of Marxism. Contrary to the espoused views of the public and their media mouthpieces, I do not subscribe to the belief that "Marxism is dead." While I am not a Marxist, I have a hard time accepting the death of something that, by its own terms, has not yet arrived. Perhaps the death of Stalinism has occurred (for the time being), but not Marxism.

Anyway, beyond my research and readings for class, life has been awfully regimented. My case load has not increased appreciably since becoming a so called junior partner (a job title) in the law firm. I still try to separate my work demeanor from my private demeanor, but I often feel it is a losing battle.

Besides work and school, I still get out for a drink or two at the Maple Leaf. The tourists have overrun the place and there is now a cover charge. I feel like a relic on occasion when I am seated at the bar and all the fresh faces come in. In fact, I thought about not returning once the cover charge was in place, but after going there for 14 or so years it is too comfortable to abandon. I need some place where I can be nobody and yet still belong, and it seems to be it. These days, however, I go less frequently. It's a minor protest on my part (one of many in this life) and the owner has given no indication that he notices or cares. I will probably go there this Saturday night to meet up with Caroline, as Rebekah will still be out of town. If it were not for Caroline I wonder if I would ever have an intelligent conversation these days.

I set my pencil down and thought about Caroline and about Rebekah, the two women in my life, one my friend and the other my lover. I had known Caroline, my friend, longer. Though it was only three plus years she and I had filled a lifetime of inquiry into those years. Rebekah was a different story, part of the riddle of more intimate relationships which I had never solved and with which I was increasingly struggling.

I drank some tea from the glass and read what I had written. I briefly became the academician critiquing student research papers. I found my explanation of the death of Stalinism not sufficiently detailed. I really meant to say a temporary death to totalitarianism masked under the name of Stalinism. I also felt the observation, denied by many, that true Marxism had not yet come into existence needed further explanation. I noted mentally that I had not mentioned the post-industrial revolution aspect, the withering away of the state, or the transition of socialism to communism.

The academician inside of me suddenly sat down at the desk inside my too often compartmentalized brain as my mind groped around for whatever else was going on in my life worth writing about. There was nothing else to mention.

I decided that I did not like what I had written but instead of tearing it up I simply pushed it to the side of the kitchen table. I took another sip of tea, swallowed slowly, and then set the glass on top of the letter and, clearing my thoughts, mindful, watched as the moisture from the bottom of the glass was absorbed in an ever-widening circle by the notebook paper. I got up to go back to bed and was happy with the thought that I would be seeing Caroline tomorrow night.

been proven," I finally responded, with certitude, looking at her over the top of my glasses. My face purposely displayed no emotion. It was her move in this ever-expanding game of access we played.

She furrowed her eyebrows down and pushed her lower lip out slightly in a frustrated frown. She had a dark sun-tanned complexion and pronounced cheek bones. Her face held all of her energy, expression and inquisitiveness. It contained the sensuality of her lips and wide eyes, the sudden anger of her arched eyebrows, the hope of her broad forehead and the purity of her smile. Her long thick black hair was braided from the top of her head down to the small of her back. The light in the bar danced furtively off sections of her hair as she, reflexively, ran her right hand down the braid to check whether it was straight on her back. A small pious white bow was affixed to the end of the braid, hiding the rubber band at the end of the braid. She was wearing a light blue cotton sun dress with darker Van Gogh blue Irises patterned across it. The dress was cut in such a modest way, almost puritan, as to reveal only that portion of her shoulder nearest her neck. She had the dress buttoned all the way up the front, with a small crucifix, almost unnoticeable, on a chain around her neck. I also noticed, during the pause in our conversation, that she was wearing a worn pair of those black ballet-type shoes, with the small brass pilgrim buckles as ornaments, that had been so popular a few years back.

"You never answered my question," she said, in a tone that made me immediately think of Saint Exupery's Little Prince, a character whom I remembered fondly never let go of a question until he had obtained an answer.

"I'm sorry, I thought it was a statement not a question," I said, wryly. Caroline raised her eyebrows again in mock annoyance at my response.

"Are you up for this?" she then asked softly. It was her polite way of assuring that I was willing to discuss a subject which might require me to focus my thoughts. It was also a tried and true method of assuring I would take the bait and allow her across the bridge.

Caroline knew me well enough to know that I had great disdain for people who made remarks like, "This is not the proper time to discuss that subject." It was a put-off, a cultural formality, which I normally equated, sometimes boisterously depending on my alcohol consumption, with the other person's lack of knowledge on the subject, or a discomfort with the validity of the position they espoused. It also, oddly, always reminded me of an adolescent admonition from my father, with which I had always privately disagreed, not to discuss politics or religion with a customer. I did not like making my intellectual curiosity subservient to someone else's standard of social etiquette. Perhaps because I grew up in a lower middle-class family, and had received no special training in the social graces in my formative years, I viewed it as a show of elitism, of an unnecessary snobbery.

To keep the moment light hearted, I decided, as I often did, to twist the intent of her question in a more prurient direction.

"I'm willing, but I may need some help keeping it up," I finally replied. She smiled and blushed, almost imperceptibly. For an intelligent woman, which she was, sex or sexually related comments by me always seemed to turn her into a sheltered fifth grade Catholic school girl. Possibly, because of her religious beliefs, which she held fervently, she had never really developed emotionally as it related to sex. She had remained, at least in my eyes, the awkward bashful fifth grader. In that regard, her attitude stood in stark contrast to the other women I had allowed to walk in and out of my life over the years.

For good or bad sex was an informal currency, the barter-
ing tool, throughout most of my indigent life prior to practicing law. It bought brief companionship, camaraderie, needed
approbation, a meal or two, and sometimes a place to stay safely
for a night. It was the only currency many of us had in our
younger poverty days. I often wondered if that really changed
as we got older, the use of it as currency, or if the trappings of
our successes simply changed the language of the barter.

The subject of sex was Caroline's Achilles heel and I knew
it. So when the mood would hit me I would gently tease her
about sex, seeking to draw her out, although not directly about
her virginity, which I found strangely admirable. I knew that
teasing her could backfire and instead of her shedding the
insecurity that I believed led to her being religious, she could,
indeed, hold on more tightly and turn away. As a result, I was
always careful to keep it lighthearted, which she allowed, and
not to go to extremes with my teasing.

However, I also knew that there was a deep individuality
in Caroline. That individuality encouraged her to wrestle with
me about religious issues and defined her boundless spiritual
nature. She was not a captive to anyone else's thinking. She did
not blindly believe everything that her religion, or any religion
for that matter, taught as dogma. Despite her strong religious
beliefs, biblically based at times, she was, for example, perfectly
willing to associate with me, the true atheist, destined, according to Judeo-Christian religions, for eternal damnation. She
was always willing to meet me in a nightclub for a drink and
although we debated religion and she challenged my beliefs,
she never proselytized. She recognized certain weaknesses in
her belief system, let me play the protagonist to point these out,
and didn't fear those weaknesses. She was, in contrast to many
others I knew who claimed to be religious, perfectly willing to
admit, discuss and explore those weaknesses. She constantly

who often taught lessons at the bar, to the dismay of the regular patrons. At the bars where Cajun music was played cliques soon developed among the new dancers, who danced only with their own groups, and, at least in my mind, the sincerity of the dance form was lost. Since the dance form had crossed that imaginary line of demarcation, out of rebellion or ill temper, I found I danced less frequently, another example of my constant need to embrace dissent.

I bought another gin and tonic for myself and ordered a Dixie beer for Phillipa. She leaned on the bar with both her elbows, sipped her beer and looking at herself in the mirror behind the bar, adjusted her hair.

"Thanks, baby," she said. "You should get out there with me and show them how it's done." I demurred.

I had met Phillipa about eight or nine years earlier when I was finishing law school. She was five or six years older than me but you would have never known it to look at her. She was one of those "near" relationships in my life, not easily seduced but seductive, the kind that you wondered about when you weren't in a relationship. She was friendly, but reticent, and left me with one memorable line uttered on a sweaty night at the Corner Bar in Breaux Bridge, the night we met and first danced to Zydeco music together: "You dance good for a white boy!" We all need good lines in life, like Appalachian trail names, bestowed by others, to help us prop up and shape our self identity. I thought of it fondly whenever I saw her.

She and I had tried to get together on two or three occasions and something had always come up to force a cancellation. As was typical for me after the slightest rebuff by a woman, real or imagined, I generally gave up pursuit.

"Have you finished the work on your Ph.D.?" I asked her.

"I just have my dissertation left," she replied, rolling the beer bottle and its moisture against her forehead to cool off. We talked for a few more minutes and then she finished the beer and left for the evening.

I glanced at the dance floor again and saw that as the band started another song, Caroline, who looked back at me, was beginning a waltz with someone else. I left the bar about thirty minutes later to try and get some sleep before going to work in the morning. Caroline walked out with me.

FOUR

~

I sat down in the chair behind my desk. Time slowed. My body was cold. My hands were closed, fingers to palm. I was suddenly conscious of the feel of the skin on my palms under my fingertips. I turned my hands over and studied the back of my hands carefully. Both hands appeared foreign to me, like I had never really seen either before. I did not recall the veins in my hands being so prominent, reminding me of my father's hands, the hands that too often harmed me as a child. I looked around my office and became aware of its exact dimensions, as if these were also new to my mind.

In front of me on my desk was a shipping invoice on a Hydro-Crane forklift. The invoice indicated that the forklift was shipped on February 11, 1979. The invoice listed the forklift's specifications, price and its serial number; JK13479M. The invoice also indicated, on its second page:

shipped without restraining belt/harness for operator.

Next to the invoice sat a copy of an affidavit prepared by me two months ago and signed by "J. Allen Meyer, Chief Engineer of Hydro Crane." The affidavit provided, at paragraph four:

Hydro-Crane forklift, serial number JK13479M,
originally shipped from our warehouse in Madison,

Wisconsin was shipped with the manufac-
turer's recommended restraining belt/har-
ness for the operator of the forklift.

The affidavit had been prepared by me at Jim Davalier's request. Davalier was the partner in our firm who dealt directly with Hydro-Crane. In light of some recent success I had with other cases, Davalier had asked me to handle the Hydro-Crane case. As a result, I had spoken directly with Mr. Meyer before drafting the affidavit. He had assured me that the forklift was shipped with a harness. I questioned him at length and he stated that he had reviewed all of the company records and it was clear that the harness had been included when the forklift was shipped. I had prepared an affidavit reflecting what he had told me.

The signed original of the affidavit had been filed by me several weeks ago with a Motion for Summary Judgment in a lawsuit against Hydro-Crane. The plaintiff in the lawsuit was injured in 1989 when he was ejected from the cab of the fork-lift as it backed off of a loading dock. The forklift had been owned by several companies since it was first shipped from the Hydro-Crane warehouse in 1979. As a result, we were attempting to rebut plaintiff's claims that the forklift had a manufacturing defect, because it had no restraining device, by proving that it did have one when it left the factory. Our argument was that at some point after shipping, one of the subsequent owners must have removed the harness and as such Hydro-Crane could not be liable for plaintiff's injuries.

A week ago, a stack of documents had made their way from Hydro-Crane to our offices. I had requested them some time prior to preparing the Motion for Summary Judgment. The company had offered excuse after excuse for the delay, to my increasing frustration, and been slow in producing the documents. In reviewing these documents, I had found the invoice. The young plaintiffs' attorney, who had only recently hung out his shingle to practice law, had never asked for the original shipping invoice in his request for production, so he was unaware of the discrepancy between the sworn affidavit and the invoice.

The hearing on the Motion for Summary Judgment was in two days. It was clear that there was an error in the affidavit. It was a critical error. I assumed that the thing to do was to withdraw the Motion. I sat at my desk for a while wondering whether Meyers had purposely given me false information, or was himself simply uninformed. Why would he lie to me and then send me the invoice which proved his lie? Perhaps the documents were sent by someone else at the company. I was also unsure of what role, if any, Davalier had played in all of this, as he had most of the client contact.

I decided to make copies of the affidavit and the conflicting invoice and give them to Davalier with a note expressing my concern. I would allow him to make the decision as to what to do. It was a cop out, but I knew that he could veto any decision I made on my own since it was his client. At that point, my only likely alternative would be to resign from the firm.

I did not believe that I had an obligation to send the invoice to plaintiff's counsel. In fact, I felt certain I could not do so. However, I felt sure that as an officer of the court, as all lawyers are, I had an obligation to withdraw the motion. I was convinced that the crucial issue in the Summary Judgment hearing would center on the affidavit and the absence, or presence, of a restraining harness at the time of shipping.

I made copies of both documents, stapled the documents together, and then attached a handwritten note to Davalier on which I wrote:

In reviewing the recently produced documents from the client, I found this invoice which contradicts the Meyer's affidavit. I think we should withdraw the Motion. What do you think?

I walked down the hall to Davalier's office and placed it on his desk. He was seated behind his desk in his most recent purchase, a brand new burgundy leather chair, with his feet up on his desk, and was talking on the phone. His cologne overwhelmed the air in his office. I returned to my office, grabbed my coat, and headed out for a walk.

I had several ethical conflicts over the years in practicing law. As a very young associate, shortly out of law school, I had steadfastly refused to work on a case representing Hooker Chemical, the polluter of Love Canal. My principled stand was met with besmirched amusement by the senior partners. Several years later I refused to represent an employer who had been sued by workers for national origin discrimination when, in our initial meeting, he referred to the Hispanic workers suing the company as "wetbacks." But being oppositional was tiring.

I walked a few blocks in each direction around the office building for about twenty minutes. My instincts told me that Davalier was not going to give me a way out. We had not worked together often, but my experience with him had not left an overall favorable impression. His reputation was as a decent trial lawyer, but I thought he was a mediocre human being. My belief, perhaps apprehension, was that he lived most of his life by covert and contradictory principles, which, I had discovered was not at all uncommon for white southern male attorneys of his generation over the age of fifty.

In our infrequent conversations, unrelated to work, when he sought to impress me with his intellect, he often embraced the stereotypical double standard between men and women and between blacks and whites, but did so under the rubric that he was agnostic and above it all, a well practiced and feigned air of indifference. Although he did not, in front of me, use terms like "nigger" or "bitch," he would make more subtle remarks about the problem of blacks taking over sports, or the supposed issue of female lawyers being "too emotional." In my mind there was no mistaking his camouflaged intent.

He also talked often about judges and other attorneys being intellectually dishonest. It was a common theme in his conversations about his disdain for the practice of law. Yet I was often told by his paralegal about the lies he would tell his wife on the phone so he could go out with whomever at night. I knew from her that he was one of too many unhappily married males whose financial success as a lawyer had brought him further, delivering a sense of entitlement, than his marriage to his high school girlfriend could ever have anticipated. It was my hope, I guess, that he really was intellectually honest and was not simply mouthing something he thought I wanted to hear. The evidence on that point, of which I was aware, was not encouraging.

I had not, however, seen him do anything that I considered unethical in his law practice, and I thought that the Hydro-Crane case presented a clear case of an ethical question. I would find out now whether the boundaries of practicing law which he talked about were, for him, real or illusory.

When I returned to my office, I found a scribbled note from Davalier, on the bottom of my handwritten note, waiting on my desk. It read:

> *It is up to the court to weigh the evidence not us. You need to simply argue the motion and affidavit—after all, as far as we know, the affidavit is correct.*

I read the note again. I thought of everything bad I had ever heard my friends say about lawyers. Maybe Shakespeare was right about killing all the lawyers. Davalier was settling into that unsavory category and now he had placed me personally in an untenable position. Was this some sort of test to co-opt me?

I was undecided on what to do. This should be easy, I thought. Davalier had essentially said that I had not seen what I had seen. Although unsure of myself, I found that I was up from my desk and walking briskly toward Davalier's office. As I entered his office he was casually watering a small Ficus tree in the corner next to a window. He slowly turned toward me.

"What's on your mind?" he asked, in a friendly tone, unconcerned, which contrasted with my seriousness. He seemed purposely oblivious to the significance of the issue I had raised. Perhaps it was an affectation. He looked back at the Ficus for a moment and gingerly removed a brown leaf. I paused.

"As best I can tell the affidavit is false," I blurted out. He slowly pulled another leaf off the Ficus and without changing his expression continued to examine the plant, with a studied interest, as he spoke to me.

"Meyers told you on the phone the affidavit was correct, didn't he?"

"Yes," I said, "but..."

"He told you he reviewed the records before signing the affidavit, correct?"

"Yes," I said. He turned away from me, relaxed, set down his brass watering can on a small credenza, and still without looking at me, moved toward his desk.

"So what's the problem?" he then asked. Again I paused, incredulous. I did not know whether to continue the discussion. It seemed obvious to me that Davalier was not going to recognize the contradiction between the affidavit and the invoice. Davalier must have sensed my uncertainty.

"I have a phone call to make," he said, unilaterally ending our discussion. As he sat down at his desk, he picked up the phone and began dialing. I turned and walked out of his office.

I returned to my office. I immediately picked up the phone and called Allen Meyers at Hydro-Crane. His secretary said he was on another line. I left a message for him to call me.

FIVE

～

I walked down the final flight of black metal stairs exiting the University of New Orleans library. I had started back in graduate school, one class a semester, a few years after I began to practice law. I had spent the better part of the evening doing research on Mikhail Bakunin's life for my graduate school political science class on Marxism. Ironically, my mind was calmed by the lack of structure in Bakunin's peripatetic life and in his barrel-chested opposition to Marx. My sojourn to the library had been a brief, but not completely successful, respite from the burgeoning stressors of work. Mikhail Bakunin's opposition to Russian imperialism, and his collectivist anarchy, was about as far removed intellectually from the confining structure of the legal practice as I could get. I looked up as I stepped into the library parking lot and noticed indifferently that the evening sky was clear. It was a warm night with scattered stars visible above Lake Pontchartrain. My calves were numb and tingled as I walked. I had not slept much last night in light of my discussion with Davalier.

I walked toward my car with one strap of my book knapsack over my right shoulder. It felt good to be just another anonymous student for a few hours. I kept my right hand under the strap near my shoulder to keep the strap from slipping off. I had a sudden urge to smoke a cigarette, something I had not done very often, except intermittently, while tending bar in college. As I walked toward the car, I thought I could taste nicotine in my mouth.

I had received a phone call earlier at work from Rebekah advising me that she was back in town and would see me at home that evening. I had not spoken to her about the Hydro-Crane forklift problem. Under the Code of Ethics, governing the legal practice and privilege, I was not supposed to discuss such things with her. For the moment it seemed like a bullshit rule to me.

I reached my car, located my keys in my knapsack, and got in the car. I looked forward to getting home. I sat down in the car and suddenly felt like I was on the verge of exhaustion. As I drove off of campus, my mind seemed to go blank for a few moments. When I became conscious of my thoughts again I did not recall the stretch of road on which I had just driven.

I pulled up in front of my house and my lethargy seemed to have a sudden adrenaline rush with the prospect of seeing Rebekah. I felt almost dizzy.

Rebekah unlocked the front door and let me into the house. I kissed her, walked past her into the house and then immediately started a rambling discourse.

"I don't think I can practice law anymore. There are just too many assholes in the legal profession...in the world for that matter." I paused and stood in the middle of the living room with my hands on my hips in theatrical defiance. Rebekah stood with her back to the front door in anticipatory silence, like someone watching a show they had seen before.

"How do they get so many assholes?" I then asked, rhetorically, as I dropped my knapsack on the living room floor and moved slowly toward the sofa to sit down. I sat for a moment, but, restless, was immediately back on my feet.

"It's an anatomical condition," Rebekah said quietly and in jest.

"I need to grow my hair longer and move to an island. I could take up the study of animals and avoid all human contact. Assholes!" I said, gesturing with both hands despairingly, as I began to walk toward the kitchen.

Rebekah had heard enough. She had an intuitive female sense, an impenetrable certainty, when it came to me, and undoubtedly to all men. Indeed, men were, on some level, nothing but grown children to her, whose every ruse she saw through and for whom she faithfully cared. Her response to my many frustrations was to assume the role of mother, sister or lover as she felt I needed. On the rare moments when I stepped outside of my personal narrative and clearly saw this characteristic displayed by her, understood my own doctrinal shallowness about others, it was humbling.

"You need a shower," she said abruptly. As I continued my incessant talking, she led me by the hand into the bathroom and took my shirt off like I was her six-year-old son who had gotten dirty once again, despite a prior parental admonition, while playing with a neighborhood friend. She was my mother at that moment, undressing me and absentmindedly nodding her head, to convey interest, every so often to something I said. She continued to undress me as I stood in front of her talking. She instructed me to lift my right leg so it would clear my pants leg as she removed them. I felt the coldness of the bathroom tile floor on my feet as she removed my socks. She pulled back the shower curtain, directed me in with a gentle wave of her hand and turned the water on. She then quickly undressed and joined me in the shower.

I stood under the showerhead and let the hot water run over my head. Rebekah rubbed some soap on a wash rag and washed my back, arms, legs and face. The irony of the situation and the tenderness that Rebekah was displaying suddenly broke through to me. I stopped talking, tried to be mindfully in the moment, and kissed her on the forehead. The adrenaline rush that had hit me outside our house was buried with the kiss. I became quiet as Rebekah slowly described her trip to me. I listened to her, a relationship skill I had admittedly not mastered.

I got out of the shower and dried myself off. Rebekah, with a towel wrapped around her torso, escorted me into the bedroom where, having temporarily exhausted my rebellion, I quickly fell asleep without any clothes on. I slept soundly, uninterrupted by troubling dreams.

When I awoke, I felt rested. It was about 4:30 a.m. and Rebekah was sleeping, breathing deeply, next to me. As I turned to face her, my movement woke her. I kissed her on the right shoulder. She turned on her side to face me and put her hand in my hair slowly rubbing my head. She moaned in a low tone as I kissed her on the neck then worked my way down to her right breast.

Rebekah pulled my hair lightly and moved my head up so that our lips touched. We kissed softly and I slipped my left hand down her body to the inside of her thighs. She rolled over onto her back pulling me with her without an awkward or wasted motion.

Sex with Rebekah was always memorable. It was a cool beer after a hot afternoon of work. It was ice cream being brought to your room as a child by a parent who had sent you to the room in punishment earlier. For some reason sex with Rebekah always lasted longer than I recalled sex having lasted with any other woman. We connected sexually on both a mental and physical level. Her body was a map I had learned well. She didn't fear exploration. Great sex, I always told myself, was impossible without a mental component. Otherwise you were just jerking off with someone else in the same room. True passion, unbridled, was humanity's feeble attempt to join together two pieces of hardened clay, to return a rib, and become a whole person. Sometimes the hardened clay pieces stuck together and sometimes not.

We started with Rebekah on the bottom, but quickly, without a wasted move, she turned me over on my back and said, in stilted fragmented words, as she started rocking back and forth on top of me, "this . . . is . . . better." As she moved back and forth on top of me with the sides of both her feet against both sides of my hip bone, I extended my arms outward and we held hands with our arms straightened and paralleling each other's bodies. Our bodies and arms formed an imperfect moving square.

Rebekah arched her lower back and threw her head back with a groan. And then slowly, the intermittent groans turned into a constant gasping for breath. Rebekah dug her nails into my hands.

After changing positions again, I lapsed off into sleep with my back dampened from beads of sweat. Rebekah's head was on my shoulder when the alarm clock went off at 6:45. We both got up and showered again in silence. I dressed and headed straight to court for the hearing on the Hydro-Crane case.

SIX

~

When the clerk called out our case number for the Hydro-Crane case, my opponent and I approached the tables by the podium in the front of the courtroom. I set my brief case on the table unopened. I walked to the podium.

"Good morning, Your Honor, Michael Tusa. I am here today on behalf of Hydro-Crane," I said dryly. I was still trying to decide what I would do.

The judge was talking to his clerk and did not acknowledge my introduction. The clerk laughed at something the judge said. I waited for the judge to turn his attention toward me before I spoke again. He finally focused his eyes on me, briefly, to tell me to begin, but then turned back to his conversation with his clerk. Any conviction I had now waned. I had read the Rules of Professional Conduct before the hearing. If the affidavit was false, and I knew it, I was clearly in violation of Rule 3.3 concerning candor towards the court.

"Your Honor, I have nothing to add by way of argument to my motion," I said. I felt nothing as I stood there. I waited a second to see if the judge had any questions, but he continued talking to his clerk. I walked back to the table and sat down. I had tried for two days to reach Allen Meyers by phone, but he had not returned my phone calls. My opponent approached the podium, introduced himself and began his argument.

Short of quitting my job, I told myself I had done all I could do by not reemphasizing the lie which I believed was in the affidavit. But it was a cop out and I knew it. The day before the hearing I had tried to convince Davalier to continue the hearing so I could speak to Allen Meyers directly, but he angrily refused and implied I would lose my job if I continued to press the issue. I realized that I was now hoping the judge would deny the motion. The judge asked my opponent a couple of questions about the affidavit. I was physically present in the room, but I felt like my spirit, seeking to disassociate from what was transpiring, was elsewhere. My opponent concluded his argument in a polite tone and the judge asked me if I had anything to add. I replied that I did not.

"All right, I have heard the argument of counsel and I have read the memorandum of both parties. It is my determination that there are no material facts at issue and the law favors defendant. Therefore, I am granting the summary judgment and will issue an order accordingly. Call the next case," the judge concluded.

I picked up my briefcase and walked away from the table. Perhaps I should have threatened to quit my job. Perhaps I should have raised the issue directly with the court, which, no doubt, might have cost me my job. My opponent came over and shook my hand. He congratulated me, but his voice rang hollow in my ears. I nodded my head as if I heard what he said.

From that day on, I felt like Davalier treated me as a co-conspirator. I had allowed my credibility to be compromised, something I never thought I would do. I felt like a phony. Thereafter, Davalier began to confide in me about his concern over his cases, disparaging judges, his clients and some of the opposing lawyers. He also tried, on occasion, to engage me in detailed conversations about his personal theories on life in general. He would go on at length about social issues with a clearly bigoted bend. I was uncomfortable, a compliant coward, but said nothing to confront him. I guess I had passed some sort of litmus test in his mind which meant it was safe to deal with me openly.

For my part, I felt terrible about the Hydro-Crane case for three or four days. Then the feeling of disgust would leave me for weeks at a time. Every so often, I would think about the Hydro-Crane case. As time went on, it was an experience to which I attached no emotional response. Intellectually, I deplored it, but my emotions could not be aroused by the recollection. I had succeeded in rationalizing my inaction.

and training," I said, in an offhanded fashion. "It has probably had a greater impact on my ability as an adult to survive in relationships," I then offered gratuitously, but without much thought, not sure why I said it.

It was funny, in a very sad sort of way, but I remembered very little of my childhood. The lack of memory would leave me for periods of time but I began to feel its nearness as if it was waiting nearby for the right moment to announce its presence more dramatically. I remembered virtually none of my childhood prior to my eleventh birthday in a first-hand way. The little I recalled prior to being eleven was like bits and pieces of a story told to me by someone else, or a faded memory of a few pages of a book long ago read, the title of which my mind repeatedly reached for but could not recall. The only reason I remembered my eleventh birthday is because that was the year that I was first thrown out of the house by my father. My mother, angry at me for some infraction---real or imagined---had called me an "idiot," a "bastard" and several other derogatory names. I thought I would be clever, my rebellion breaking through, and, as I walked away from her, and in front of my father, pointed out that she had forgot to call me a "moron." I have the faintest recollection of running and hurdling the backyard fence with my father in outraged pursuit. He failed to catch me. I contemplated walking to my grandmother's house but it was late, near dark, and she lived miles away. So I went around the corner to my friend Keith's house.

Ultimately, later that night, my friend's mother, in hushed tones, called my father on the phone and he drove over to pick me up. He blew the horn, perhaps embarrassed, while sitting in the car in front of my friend's house. As I closed the car door behind me he said one of those other lines I will always remember, another part of my identity: "I just want you to know that I'm only doing this because your mother wants you theory, but even if that is the proper generalization from my specific comments regarding you, what's wrong with them?"

"Well, for one thing, it means essentially that there is no such thing as free will," I replied. "I did not choose my parents, or the childhood difficulties visited on me, yet the environment of that childhood, which I did not control, under your theory, completely dictates my religious belief or non-belief. I'm unwilling to blame them, if that's the right word, for my beliefs." I paused. "And it sounds a little like a psychological version of Martin Luther's predestination. I'm damned without my input. And if there is a God who pairs us with parents who will inflict such pain as to lead to non-belief in Him, what does that say about such a God?" I asked. Caroline thought for a long moment and then countered.

"We are all programmed to some degree by our parents. I admit that. We're prisoners of their mistakes and their successes. I don't see how you can argue against that fact. But you seem to be suggesting those parental mistakes are irrelevant to who we become." Her head rose off of her knees as she finished speaking and a look of genuine concern, spanning unseen generations, was etched on her face. She made me promise that the discussion would eventually return to the particular case study of myself before responding to my free will comment and I agreed.

"Our childhood is not irrelevant. You are right," I replied. "But I have to believe I can reason myself past it; otherwise, I have no free will and my adult life is pre-ordained."

"I don't believe we have complete free will anyway, but I do believe we exercise free will within certain God given parameters," she said, fleshing out the combination of words to see if these fit together.

"Sounds like a new theory called relative free will," I said with a chuckle. "Actually, I believe the Catholics have

the market cornered on that notion." As I spoke, somewhere in my mind I recalled Bertrand Russell in *The ABC's of
Relativity* chastising his readers for saying "everything is relative."
If everything is relative, I seem to recall him writing, there is
no absolute to which anything could be relative. I never understood much else of what Russell had written in the book.
The theory of relativity was something, like the predilections of
the few rich women I had dated after becoming a lawyer, that
I never understood. Caroline smiled slightly at my comment
about Catholics, but did not laugh.

"I think your belief in relative free will, and your proposal
that childhood experiences completely preordain religious convictions, or lack thereof, may be in conflict," I said.

"No more so than your belief in absolute free will, and your
belief, as you said a few moments ago, that you know nothing
objectively. I assume that you know nothing objectively because
you are subjectively bound by your own experiences and those
subjective bonds are impediments to your exercise of free will,"
she replied quickly and sternly. She had the better of me on
that point and she knew it.

I, again, had a flash in my mind of something I had once
read. My mind seemed to work that way, looking for anchors,
understanding, in other people's words. I recalled vaguely that
the psychologist gad-fly Thomas Szasz had written that the
party who succeeds at defining a given situation wins. I knew
that there were weaknesses in my existential belief in absolute
free will. Caroline was properly pointing this out.

William James had written in a diary entry that "my first
act of free will shall be to believe in free will." Maybe, in the
end, that's all free will really is, just a decision to believe in it.
However, since I felt that we are all absolutely responsible for
our own actions, anything less than complete free will jeop-
ardized that pivotal element of the belief system which I had

constructed. Where did my strident need for absolute free will and responsibility come from? What was it tied to? Caroline closed her eyes as if lost in thought or prayer. I yawned.

"I think we have reached a very definitive conclusion here," I then offered. "And the conclusion is that we are both inconsistent." Caroline opened her eyes slowly and with a delighted look, showing two rows of perfectly ordered white teeth, laughed. She straightened her legs back out on the sofa, turned her back to me and in laying down, placed a small pillow and then her head on my lap.

"All right, now we can talk about your particular case," she said, looking up fondly at me. I buried half of my face on the arm of the sofa in mock frustration.

"Wake me up when it's my turn to answer," I said, out of the side of my mouth. She dug her fingernails lightly and affectionately into my arm. After a long discussion Caroline dressed and left the house as Rebekah returned.

EIGHT

~

W ill you zip up my suitcase for me while I call the photographer?" Rebekah asked, in a voice from the other room.

I got off the sofa in the living room, dutifully, without answering, and walked into the bedroom where her suitcase was sitting on the edge of the bed. Rebekah was seated on the bed near the nightstand. She leaned cross legged toward the nightstand and began to dial a number on the phone. I slowly zipped up the suitcase, pausing periodically to fold and push shirt sleeves and pants' legs out of the zipper's path.

"I thought this was only a two-day trip," I stated, somewhat playfully to Rebekah. Rebekah looked at me with the phone against her ear and responded to my comment by sticking her tongue out.

"Hello, David," she said, turning away from me. "Our plane arrives at 7:15 p.m. Its Delta 247. Can you still pick us up?"

I finished zipping up the suitcase, lifted it off the bed, placed it on the floor in an upright position and walked back out of the room while Rebekah continued her conversation on the phone. I returned to the sofa and located my place in *The Catcher in the Rye*. I could still hear Rebekah's voice in the background, but could no longer make out what she was saying.

I had read *The Catcher in the Rye*, and the exploits of Holden Caulfield, three or four times since turning fifteen. I always found the book oddly reaffirming and had reread it on several occasions when I felt things were too chaotic in my life, though I'm not sure I understood the specific motivation each time. There was an emotional attachment, a sense of belonging, to the book which was hard for me to explain. I found that I also reread *The Little Prince* and occasionally *Through the Looking Glass*. Perhaps, for me, these three books together represented a replacement for the lost memories of my childhood.

Rebekah hung up the phone and came into the living room. She sat next to me on the sofa and, pulling her legs up, assumed a yoga like position with the soles of her feet touching and her heels near her groin. She was wearing a short yellow skirt with no pantyhose. I wondered if she had underwear on, but continued to give the impression I was engrossed in my book. I could not recall seeing her get dressed in the morning.

"Our flight arrangements are finalized. David is going to pick us up at the San Diego airport tonight," Rebekah said. I nodded my head to her statement, still giving the appearance that I was only half listening. "We'll need to leave for the airport in about 45 minutes," she said, as she rubbed the back of her neck. I was hesitant about this trip. I needed a break but I was already struggling with the requirements of being in a relationship. But, I thought, I would press forward and maybe the restlessness would pass.

"Honey, do you think Holden Caulfield is crazy?" I then asked, holding my thumb in the book as a marker, as I looked over at her.

Rebekah paused and then, after thinking about it, replied that she wasn't sure, she would have to read the book again. She opined that whether he was crazy or not, she felt that he was not representative of her thoughts or her experiences as an adolescent.

"But, I know you feel different," she said, in a conciliatory tone. She lowered her hands into the enclave of her lap.

We had conversations about Holden Caulfield on several other occasions. She had remarked previously that she was somewhat unnerved with my apparent preoccupation with the book and the character of Holden Caulfield. Her memory of the book's content was limited, but she always equated it with the murder of John Lennon. She was not possessive of me, or my time, in general, but she was somewhat insecure with my affinity to what she considered to be a novel of marginal significance.

"You're not sixteen anymore," she would say, unsuccessfully, but tentatively, to try to break my bond with the book.

I was fairly comfortable with my enjoyment of the book. It was a point of reference for me that allowed me, on a periodic basis, to determine the extent to which I had abandoned the honesty of my adolescence for the intolerance and "phoniness" of being an adult. I was all too painfully aware, at this point in my life, of how far away from my perceptions of childhood purity my life had taken me. Perhaps it was just a nostalgic attachment on my part.

I often thought of J. D. Salinger, the author of *The Catcher in the Rye,* and his living for years in self-imposed isolation and I would discuss this idea with Rebekah as well, because I too had always thought that I would just disappear one day. I wasn't exactly sure where I would disappear to, or even exactly what it meant to disappear, but the idea had always had a hold on me.

In Salinger's case, he had created a character, Holden Caulfield, that, in some ways, set the limits of his public existence. He could not become involved with society, attend dress up banquets, accept awards, give public interviews, without betraying that part of him that was Caulfield. So he lived like a hermit, writing books that might be published after he died, when he, as Holden Caulfield, would be immune from any criticism.

Rebekah would correctly note in such discussions about the book that children could be quite cruel and it was a misrepresentation to assert that the child's perspective was always angelic. She would recount stories from her own childhood about the mean things childhood friends had done to her, or to classmates. I marveled at her recollection of these childhood incidents which were in contrast to my complete lack of a childhood memory. As to her comments about *The Catcher in the Rye*, I could never tell, however, how much of her criticism of the book was of its contents and how much was directed at her discomfort over my attachment to it.

The book was part of a comfort zone to me. I suspect that in my adolescence it provided me with an affirmation, of certain thoughts, which I could not receive elsewhere. Rereading the book, even years later, took me back to the memory of the happy discovery of that childhood connection.

"Do you have underwear on?" I asked, as flirtatious as I could. Rebekah's eyes widened and she arched her eyebrows slipping her fingers over the hem of her skirt and lifting it slightly as a tease.

"Who wants to know? You or Holden Caulfield?" she responded.

"Both of us," I replied, recalling that Holden, on page 63, had indicated that sex was something he really didn't understand.

As I lowered myself onto the floor in front of her, and Rebekah, who remained seated on the sofa, unfolded her legs, I guessed that Holden would have been mortified.

NINE

~

I settled into the seat next to the window over the wing of the airplane. Rebekah was seated next to me. The cabin slowly pressurized and within minutes the familiar repetitive whine of the head stewardess about the safety features of the airplane began.

Rebekah had a two-day modeling job in San Diego and I needed a break from the strain of work and could take a few days off before having to prepare for my next trial. It would in essence allow us to take a long weekend in San Diego. Rebekah had told me I could come to the modeling shoot once we were in San Diego, but I had remained noncommittal. I would often refuse to commit to doing something with her that involved other people until the last minute. Actually I found that I had that habit with everyone I knew. For some reason I felt that I needed to live my life with the assurance that I could always walk away from anyone, or any situation, without notice, as the need arose. Was that, in some way, related to my longing to disappear, to go where no-one knew me? Or did I simply resist anything that looked like submission?

I thought, in this case, that I might just wander around the city for a while without a schedule of any type; that was my preferred way to visit a city. The shoot was for a cosmetic company and, as I gathered, would focus the camera exclusively on Rebekah's face and various makeup approaches.

I turned to look at that face and saw that Rebekah was transfixed by the stewardess's mindless routine concerning the proper procedure for using an oxygen mask. Rebekah's physical beauty was remarkable. She had strawberry blonde hair, blue eyes, and that slightly too white skin of natural redheads. I searched her face for wrinkles and saw none. She noticed me staring, with the recent glow of lovemaking, and turned and met my glance briefly.

It was another exchange of looks between lovers, words conveyed without speaking. I recalled briefly that early in our relationship Rebekah and I had this ability to communicate without speaking, at least about sexual matters. A glance between us relayed a desire to move from the bed to the floor, or to change positions. Her look, the slight arch of an eyebrow, a dip of her chin, now relayed to me that I was crazy, there were too many people on the plane to even think about trying. There would be no attempt to become members of the "mile high" club.

As Rebekah turned her glance back to the stewardess and her concluding safety remarks, I found myself daydreaming about different places where I had sex with women over the years. I could not decide whether such grouping of thoughts was sexist. Perhaps it was only sexist if I said the thoughts out loud. I, however, was never quite sure where the line delineating sexist thoughts or remarks began. Some things were obvious to me, others were not. I dismissed my brief politically correct concern over what social deficiencies such thoughts might reflect.

In thinking back on these things, I again looked at Rebekah who had begun to thumb through a magazine. We had met one night when I was out with Norman, an amiable lawyer I had tried a case against. She was out with two female friends and Norman was in hot pursuit of all three of them.

I tagged along remarkably apathetic, considering the attractiveness of Rebekah and her two friends. Or, perhaps, I was experimenting with a lesson from my college bartending days, which was that the best way to catch a woman was not to try. At some point, the caravan, over my objection, made its way to a neon-lit discotheque. I veered away from the group to a seat at the bar. After a drink or two, I tired of waiting for Norman to give up the chase and asked the bartender to call me a cab. No sooner were the words out of my mouth, when I realized Rebekah was beside me and she asked if I would like her to give me a ride home. I accepted the offer, we spent the night together, and a month later she moved in with me.

I looked out the window of the plane. It was well above New Orleans now. I could see the meandering course of the Mississippi River and tried unsuccessfully to orient myself to the geography below. I gave up, adjusted my seat back and closed my eyes.

TEN

~

When I returned to our hotel room, after walking alone around San Diego, I noticed that the phone light was blinking indicating that there was a message. Rebekah had called to tell me that she would be at the photograph shoot until about 5:00 p.m. The message indicated that she wanted to me to meet her and some "new friends" for dinner at 6:00. She left me the restaurant's name and address. I looked at the clock on the night stand and it showed 3:15. I thought briefly about taking a nap, but decided instead to go downstairs to the hotel bar.

Surprisingly, for the time of day, the bar was crowded. There was a convention of some type at the hotel as numerous people were walking about with those cheap stick-on name tags. I seated myself at the far end of the bar so I could see people entering. It was a habit that I learned from my Sicilian grandfather whose only advice to me as a teenager was to never sit anywhere in public with your back to the door. No-one ever shot at me but, presumably, for him it made good occupational sense. Even if it served no purpose for me it had been inculcated in me along some generational line. My father, without explanation to me, had followed the same advice.

I thought briefly of my grandfather who had come to America by boat at age 13 with his 6 year old brother. Just the two of them. He had died nearly ten years ago at the age of 93. His last years were disquieting for him as his mind still functioned well, but his body had tired of the fight for survival and had decided to abandon him. As a result, non-ambulatory and incontinent, he was painfully aware of the fact that he was unable to take care of himself. Perhaps this was a karmic punishment for the abuse he had visited upon his own children.

As an adolescent, I had often heard my father and his brothers, my uncles, discuss how brutal my alcoholic grandfather had been to them as kids. These stories were always told with humor and lots of laughter, an ill-formed defense that they had all developed to the abuse. As a young teenager I'm not sure I understood the strange dichotomy between the horrors of the stories and the laughter, but, unaware, I laughed along with them. My observations of my elderly grandfather, when my father and I visited him each Sunday, were, in stark contrast, of a peaceful, gentle but superstitious man, with little formal education, always cooking large pots of red gravy; what Sicilians called pasta sauce. I never reconciled these two images of the man; the brutal and the peaceful. Perhaps we are made up of such contradictions, as exemplified by the contradictions and obligations between being a father and being a grandfather.

His marriage to my grandmother had been prearranged by their families while they were both children and still living in Sicily. He brought my grandmother to America when he had enough money to pay for her passage. He never remarried after my grandmother's early death in her 50s and, whatever his real reason, explained his decision by telling me that he couldn't remarry as he would then have two wives in heaven.

As some of the bar patrons came closer, I was able to read their name tags. From the bartender, I learned that it was a convention of romance novelists. I was struck, however, with the fact that the majority of those with name tags were women.

Although I had never read a romance novel I instinctively had little respect for the genre. On the literary ladder it was one rung above fuck books, which in my mind put it on the same rung as "The National Enquirer." What is the use of the genre? At best it resulted in people reading something, even if the substance was lacking. At worst it perpetuated dull stereotypes, required no thinking, and gave a false read on life. Maybe it was just another needed distraction.

I didn't know if my disdain was misplaced arrogance, or simply a reflection of my suspicion of anything which became popular to the public. It was a weakness of the mind, or an attachment to a materialist world view which made people follow the herd, I thought. My life had to be ordered by me, not dictated by popular culture. At least that is how I rationalized my self-image.

The seats at the bar filled up. The novelists, or would be novelists, were now seated on both sides of me. The woman on my right was engaged in a conversation with her companion about another romance writer. From the bits and pieces of the conversation I was able to hear she thought the latest novel by the novelist they were discussing was trash.

"I don't care if it's a good story. She completely violated the formula," I heard her say.

The woman on my left sat alone at the bar. I noticed with a glance that her name tag read, "Hi, I'm CAROL."

As it turned out, Carol was a would-be novelist. She had a Masters in English Literature from the University of Colorado and had been unsuccessful at finding an agent, or getting her first two novels of fiction published. As a result she thought she might try her hand at a romance novel. She admitted that she was a bit uncomfortable in the company of the other convention attendees, but felt she had learned a little about the formulaic writing styles for romance novels from the conference.

We spent some time talking about our favorite authors and books. She was a fan of Alice Walker. I told her I had read *Possessing the Secret of Joy*. I was surprised that she had read Charles Bukowski's *Women* and found it an "interesting style." I needed to leave but was not excited about doing so. Carol was a good conversationalist and I found I suddenly resented having to alter my schedule to meet Rebekah. We talked for a while longer and then I headed off, a few minutes late, to meet Rebekah and her friends for dinner.

ELEVEN

~

Rebekah was seated at a round table in the middle of the restaurant. There were two guys seated at the table with her. I saw her laugh, somewhat insincerely, at something one of the guys said. She looked up and saw me approaching. Her eyes seemed to widen and she stood and kissed me when I reached the table. She looked beautiful as always, but I could tell the night was not going to go well. I felt resistance building within myself.

Her two dinner guests both worked for the company that was involved in filming the models. One was named Gary and the other Lofton. The one named Lofton, for reasons that were not made clear to me, went by the nickname "Cat" and was a photographer. Both were tanned, well groomed and well dressed. Instinctively, I didn't like them.

After brief introductions the conversation at the table centered mostly on Cat's perception that photographers were always being asked to compromise their integrity by product sponsors. As an example he referred to the fact that he had to use Elmer's glue when he needed to film milk for an ad because the glue was whiter than the milk and made a better appearance on film. I listened politely, but did not participate in the conversation. Rebekah glanced at me once or twice to convey her concern that I was being nonresponsive. I tried to look interested and to laugh at the appropriate time throughout the conversation. However, since I had no interest in what was being discussed, I suspect my timing was off by a second or two.

At some point during a lull in the conversation Gary asked me if there were similar problems in the practice of law. I knew that there were, but simply, with a formless apathy, indicated "sometimes." When everyone at the table waited for me to fill in the details, I did not. After a moment Rebekah began asking Cat about something that had occurred during the afternoon session.

The only time during the evening that I contributed to the conversation was when Cat volunteered that he was an agnostic because, he said a bit too cheerfully, "one can never know." I laughed, sensing that this comment was a tried and true one which he normally made to distinguish himself. Everyone stopped to determine why I was laughing. I set my drink down.

"I'm sorry I was laughing at your agnostic remark."

"Are you an agnostic also?" Cat asked, as if he was hopeful of discovering that I was a former fraternity brother. I laughed again, but more sarcastically. He seemed confused.

"No, I'm not," I said happily. "Agnosticism, really, in my opinion, is such crap." Rebekah looked at me sternly, but I ignored her. "By definition it states one can neither know or believe that there is or is not a God, and that is such a silly position to take on such an important subject. I think it really means a person doesn't want to think about it." I raised my glass to drink the last of my gin and thought for a moment of Caroline and my desire to be talking to her. The ice in the glass fell forward dripping some liquid on my chin. I wiped it away with my hand as I set my glass down.

"Do you study philosophy?" Gary asked, in what I took as a placating manner. I avoided his question and turned my unfettered disdain to Cat.

"An agnostic is someone who either does not have the balls to make a decision, or enough desire to look into the issues further. It's really a fucking cop out," I said, swinging wide of the mark. Cat did not respond. Rebekah was tense.

"Tell us how you really feel," Gary said, half joking, and turned to look at Cat, who was sullen, as if unprepared for a challenge to what he had said.

"You can neither prove nor disprove the existence of a God, so agnosticism seems a reasonable position to me," Cat finally said, slightly disillusioned and without much conviction. I realized at that moment I should have played the good boyfriend and let the matter go, but I could not do it. I had the overwhelming sense, rightly or wrongly, that most people were terrible phonies who mouthed platitudes and descriptors which they had not really thought out. Cat, through no fault of his own, was in the cross-hairs of my often unfocused and unnecessary anger on the subject.

"You can't prove or disprove the existence of love can you? Does it exist? Do you understand the distinction between knowing something and believing something or is it all the same to you?" I asked, leaning confrontationally, in cross examination, across the table. Rebekah placed her hand on my arm, as if she feared I was about to get up.

"Of course, I understand the distinction...," he started to say.

"Are you telling me that there is no basis, from studying and contemplation, to either know that a God exists, or to form a reasonable belief that a God exists?" I asked, more gently as I leaned back. Cat looked at Gary uneasy.

"Exactly," he said, smiling uneasily and clasping his hands together.

"And by definition you are also saying that there is no basis for knowing there is no God, or for forming a reasonable

belief that there is no God, correct?" I then asked. I was being
too dogmatic, the opposite sin of apathy, but I didn't care. Cat
remained silent, not ready for the assault.

"I'd like to study some philosophy some day," Gary then
said, rescuing his friend. I sat back completely in my chair and,
without regard for those at the table, looked for the waitress so
I could order another drink. Rebekah, to diffuse the situation
I had created, then interjected something about fashion and a
lively inane conversation between the three of them ensued.

I was pleased when the meal was finally over and Rebekah
and I headed back to the hotel. While in the taxi Rebekah
turned to face me and for several long seconds just looked at
me, wounded, with pain and disapproval, as she held my hand.
I slowly turned toward her.

"What?" I asked, stupidly, knowing full well what she was
concerned about, but unable to confront my own behavior; a
behavior that I still did not understand.

"If what people are talking about is not important to
you, you just won't participate will you. And why must you
attack anyone who does not believe what you believe?" she
asked. I knew that she was talking about the conversation over
dinner, but did not immediately respond. "You were completely
withdrawn and antisocial. I don't think you realize how often
you do that," she said coldly, releasing my hand. I apologized
to her, and in an offhanded manner told her I had a lot on my
mind and wanted to get to bed early since our flight out was
early in the morning. I was dodging the issue. I knew, however, that she was right, but I felt no remorse. I had belittled
her friend, thrown the first punch, and then withdrew into
myself rather than participate in conversation about the topics
of interest to them. I had no desire to engage either of her
friends in conversation and so I did not. It was not the socially
acceptable thing to do.

Once back at the hotel, I undressed in the inflamed quiet and quickly went to bed. Although there was no reason to do so, I childishly turned my back to Rebekah to sleep. It took me a long time to fall asleep, but I did not move, as if to prove to her that I fell asleep effortlessly and with a clear conscience.

She was right. I was completely withdrawn and anti-social. So I tried to use the opportunity to examine how I had gotten to that point. As I lay in bed I asked myself questions and answered them as best I could. I knew that throughout my life I could drop the curtain on my emotions without warning. I became robotic, almost like a long suffering prisoner of war dulling his emotions so as to avoid the pain of the unpleasant past memories. I knew I did it when I felt I was about to be hurt, but I also knew that I did it on countless other occasions when there appeared to be no threat to me. And why the hostility, the need to prove that I was right at the expense of another? What caused this? Where did this characteristic need for approbation, or attention, come from? I felt like I was trying to catch and hold smoke.

The next morning we flew home, cordial but distant. I had offended Rebekah, but she appeared to forgive me. For good or bad I had another trial the following week and knew I would be immersed in trial preparation, leaving little time for thinking further about my behavior.

TWELVE

~

I walked quickly down the hall toward my office. It was 7:00 a.m. and I assumed that the offices would be empty. From a side door, Davalier suddenly stepped out into the hall. Seeing me, he smiled slightly. His tie was loose and his coat appeared slept in. I thought I detected a hint of inebriation in his eyes.

"Morning," he said. I nodded in recognition, but did not respond. Despite my physical presence in the office, I was mentally preoccupied with thoughts about the *Masterson* trial scheduled to start at 8:30 a.m. The trial concerned my client's claim for damages for work done on an offshore project prior to being fired from the job. The defendant, Mire Enterprises, claimed my client, Masterson Electrical, had performed no work of any value as of the time of its removal.

I had developed the ability to focus intensely on a subject when necessary and used that focus often when involved in litigation. It was as if I suppressed everything else in my life during the duration of the litigation. Inevitably when the litigation was over, and the dragon of ambition slain, there was a tremendous, inexplicable, emotional letdown.

As I walked past where Davalier stood, he spoke further. "If you have some time this afternoon I have a case I want to discuss with you."

I grunted out an "OK" and walked into my office. I knew that I would be in trial all day but did not tell him because I did not feel like engaging him in conversation.

All of my exhibits for the trial were already packed in my car. I did, however, need to pick up some photograph blow-ups and a chart which, hopefully, my secretary Melinda had picked up the evening before when I was out of the office preparing witnesses. I found these wrapped in brown paper and leaning against my credenza. On the top of the package was a yellow stick-em note with "Good luck" written on it. I made a mental note to thank Melinda later. I picked up the package and placed it under my arm. I visually scanned my office to be sure I was not missing anything. I then hurriedly walked out recalling that I promised the client I would meet him at 8:00 a.m. at the courthouse.

THE COURT: Okay. Good morning. I'm sorry about our late start today. Please be seated. Call the case please.

THE CLERK: Civil Action 92-3611, Masterson Electrical versus Mire Enterprises.

THE COURT: Counsel, enter your appearances for the record please.

MR. TUSA: Michael Tusa on behalf of the plaintiff, Masterson Electrical.

MR. KASTE: James Kaste on behalf of the defendant, Mire Enterprises.

THE COURT: Okay. Thank you. Are both sides ready to go forward?

MR. TUSA: Plaintiff is ready, Your Honor.

MR. KASTE: Defendant is also ready, Your Honor.

THE COURT: Does either party desire a sequestration order?

MR. KASTE: Yes, Your Honor.

THE COURT: Would the witnesses come forward, please? Gentlemen, the parties have requested a sequestration of the witnesses. And, basically, what that means is that we're going to ask you to leave the courtroom and to talk to no one other than your lawyers, either Mr. Kaste or Mr. Tusa, regarding this case or any fact which might be relevant to this case, until this trial is over. You may not talk amongst yourselves about the case. OK. You may talk about anything else you wish, the Saints football team, the governor's race, any jokes or anything else like that but not this case. Okay? Thank you.

MR. TUSA: Your Honor, we are designating Mr. Edward Gandie as the company representative.

THE COURT: Okay. You may stay Mr. Gandie.

MR. KASTE: Your Honor, we designate Steven Fontes as the company representative for Mire Enterprises.

MR. TUSA: Your Honor, Mr. Fontes does not work for the defendant in this case, so I'm curious upon which grounds he is being designated as a company representative.

MR. KASTE: I don't think there's any requirement that—that—Judge, he does work for the parent corporation of Mire Enterprises.

MR. TUSA: Your Honor, Rule 615 of the Rules of Evidence indicates that in order for someone to be present, they have to either be a party to the lawsuit or a person whose presence is shown by a party to be essential to the presentation of the party's cause. My appreciation, Judge, is that Mr. Fontes has no personal knowledge of the work at issue in this case and so how can he be essential? But perhaps I'm wrong.

THE COURT: Is Mr. Fontes going to testify?

MR. KASTE: Well, yes, he is. He is the person who compiled the contract documents in this case.

THE COURT: Mr. Tusa I have never had this issue raised before by counsel. Although, it is a legitimate issue for you to raise. What proof, if any, must Mire Enterprises show to prove Mr. Fontes is essential to the presentation of their case?

MR. TUSA: Your Honor, just to make this easy, if Mr. Kaste says that Mr. Fontes is essential to his presentation of the case then I'll back off.

THE COURT: Mr. Kaste?

MR. KASTE: He is very important, uh, essential to our case.

THE COURT: Good enough Mr. Tusa?

MR. TUSA: Yes, Your Honor.

THE COURT: Okay. I'm going to allow him to stay as a corporate representative under the authority of section 3 of Rule 615 and that's based on Mr. Kaste's assurance to me that Mr. Fontes' presence is essential to the presentation of his case. Now, if in the testimony, we find that's not correct, we have a mistrial at Mire Enterprises' expense.

I returned to my chair at the conference table and picked up a notepad. I was pleased with the Judge's statement and my opponent's affirmation that Mr. Fontes' testimony was essential. Kaste's client had pulled a fast one by announcing several days before trial that the general manager of Mire who had supervised the job was out of the country and would not be present at trial. They had previously assured me the general manager would be at the trial and had listed him as a "will-call" witness. As it was a judge trial the record would be left open and the general manager's testimony would be entered by deposition. I feared the general manager would have the advantage of being briefed on what had occurred at the trial prior to having to give his deposition. My plan, therefore, was to call Fontes as a witness and ask him a variety of questions about areas I was sure he would not be prepared to answer. In order to emphasize any advantage I might gain with this tactic, I wanted it clear in the record that Fontes was considered "essential" so my opponent might feel restricted about objecting that my areas of inquiry were outside Fontes' knowledge.

I was also hopeful that Fontes' ego would get in his way and he would try to answer questions to which he should indicate lack of knowledge. There were so many exhibits in this case, more than 120, that I felt certain Fontes would not be well versed on all on them.

I called my first witness, Edward Gandie, the president of the company. Prior to the trial I had been somewhat concerned about how Gandie would do as a witness. In our trial preparation, he spent more time talking about his experiences during the Korean War than his company's claim for $220,000.00 in lost profit due to Mire's cancellation of the contract. During those meetings, I often thought of my father, a former marine who fought in Korea. I had developed a great admiration for the soldier in the field as a result of countless camp fire stories and much reading. I had also realized, years later, when I thought of the romanticized and comic nature of those stories, that Phil Caputo, the author of *A Rumor of War*, was right; the problem with war was there was no background music. The romanticized nature of war that we had heard about growing up, I had learned, was a politicized story to make it more palatable for the masses and nothing more.

Despite my concerns, Gandie turned out to be a very credible witness. He was well prepared for my direct examination. As I had instructed him, he was very animated and made frequent eye contact with the Judge.

The cross-examination of Gandie was uneventful. The few points made by my opponent were easily corrected on redirect. Because of the numerous exhibits, however, Gandie was on the stand nearly 4 hours. The Judge advised us that she had a criminal docket set for the late afternoon so it was decided to break at the conclusion of Gandie's testimony.

I met briefly with Gandie and my other witnesses after the day's testimony and we agreed to meet in the courtroom at 8:30 the next morning. As I left the courthouse I had a flash of the lyrics to a John Prine song:

We lost Davy in the Korean War,
I still don't know what for,
it doesn't matter anymore.

THIRTEEN

~

MR. TUSA: Your Honor, we call Steven Fontes as our next witness.

THE COURT: Okay.

THE CLERK: Please have a seat and state your name for the record.

THE WITNESS: My name is Steven C. Fontes.

MR. TUSA: Good morning, Mr. Fontes.

I could tell by Fontes' expression that he was somewhat surprised by my calling him to the witness stand. As he stood to walk to the witness stand he had looked at Kaste to see if Kaste had some objection to make. Kaste seemed unaware of his witness's concerns and occupied himself by searching for a document at his table. After Fontes was sworn in and a proper foundation for the questions was laid I immediately turned my questioning to Mire's principal defense and the language of a variety of documents.

MR. TUSA: And, so is it Mire's position in this litigation that nothing done by Masterson on this job was completed prior to Mire canceling the contract?

MR. FONTES: There was nothing of any beneficial use to us.

MR. TUSA: I appreciate that personal observation but my question is, was there anything that Masterson did on the job which was completed prior to the cancellation of the contract?

MR. FONTES: No parts of the contract were completed.

MR. TUSA: Do you know if Mire Enterprises ever represented to GCE, the company which replaced Masterson on the job, that Masterson had completed certain portions of the work?

MR. FONTES: I have no firsthand knowledge of that.

MR. TUSA: Why don't you take a look at Exhibit 43 Mr. Fontes. Is that a copy of the subcontract entered into between Mire Enterprises and GCE?

MR. FONTES: Yes, sir. It is.

MR. TUSA: And there are some construction procedures attached to this contract, correct?

MR. FONTES: Yes, sir.

MR. TUSA: And this subcontract and these construction procedures were prepared by Mire Enterprises, correct?

MR. FONTES: Yes, sir.

MR. TUSA: Please take a look at paragraph 4 on page 6 of the subcontract. . . . Why don't you read that out loud sir?

MR. FONTES: "It will not be necessary to frame up the interior of floors 6-10 as this was completed by Masterson Electrical."

MR. TUSA: So, Mire did represent to GCE that Masterson had completed the interior of floors 6-10?

MR. FONTES: Well, the document says that—

MR. TUSA: Please take a look at Exhibit 41 sir.

MR. FONTES: Yes, sir I see it.

MR. TUSA: This is a letter from the general manager of your company to Mr. Thompson at GCE, correct?

MR. FONTES: Yes, sir.

MR. TUSA: And this letter was sent out to GCE when Mire Enterprises was trying to find a replacement for Masterson on the job, correct?

MR. FONTES: I think so.

MR. TUSA: And on the second page of this letter at paragraph 3, it states that Masterson Electrical had completed all of the electrical wiring in floors 6-10 and there was no need to redo this work, correct?

MR. FONTES: You would have to ask the general manager about that.

MR. TUSA: That's what the letter says isn't it?

MR. KASTE: Objection, the document speaks for itself.

MR. TUSA: Eloquently, I might add.

THE COURT: The document is clear. Move on.

The examination of Fontes continued for the remainder of the day. We discussed, in one fashion or another, 33 different exhibits with Fontes. It all went well and when the trial ended the judge read her opinion from the bench awarding my client the damages requested.

There is nothing like a good cross examination at a trial. In order to pull it off one must be well prepared. Indeed, the attorney needs to know the overall facts better than any single witness. You never ask a question you do not already know the answer to and can prove. I have often thought that in preparing for a trial I am preparing a play in which I must not only know all of the actor's lines but must force them to recite, even when they do not want to remember their lines. It is satisfying when it all comes together, but for me, there was always the inevitable let down upon completion.

FOURTEEN

~

The nights since the trial had begun to run together on me; a broad damp feeling that an indefinable gnawing dread was overwhelming me.

I had been at this disconnected place before in my life and knew its familiar hazy terrain, even if I did not know the cause. It was a place where feeling indifferent, remote and flat, was accepted as normal; where working hours and sleeping hours bled into each other and were scrambled without clear reason; where my meal times changed, or were simply missed when I had no appetite. Inertia was my primitive waking companion. It was hard to be focused on anything in particular and my life was lived barely, alone, waiting, until something, some extreme where I could feel again, set me off. It was not a safe place to be.

I looked up at my image in the mirror behind the bar. The mirror was part of the heavy mahogany bar set that was at least fifty years old. The glass in the mirror was faded and spotted in the corners from moisture. On either side of the bar mirror were the pressed aluminum sheets which served as the wall and ceiling covering. It was an old New Orleans' neighborhood bar combination that I found reassuring. Like most people, when the present or future was uncertain I sought solace in the nostalgia of an imagined unchanging past.

I had been to the Maple Leaf so many nights in a row since the *Masterson* trial that I realized that I couldn't recall which bands had played on which nights. Caroline was at the bar. She had come by for an hour or two some nights to "check on me," as she described it. Rebekah stayed at home, worried, choosing to keep her distance from something she did not understand and which I did not have the words to explain to her. Caroline and I had conversations each night, but I couldn't recall much of the substance of the conversations. Mostly she would just sit with me and, on occasion, when the impulse hit her, dance with someone and ask me to watch.

It was about 1:00 a.m. I guessed. I did not know for sure since I did not wear a watch; another of my long-standing objections to social conformity. There was, thankfully, no clock on any wall in the bar. If my guess was correct, I had to be at work in seven hours. I did not like the way my image looked in the mirror. Although I generally pretended to pay little attention to my appearance, an apathetic facade, I thought my face looked too thin. I could see my cheekbones and my jaw-bone highlighted in the shadows on my face. I needed a shave before the start of the Monday workweek. I looked at myself in the mirror as if I was looking at someone else's features. I sometimes had that odd feeling that I was outside of my body, separated, observing my own behavior from afar. I wondered if that feeling was unique to me, or if other people had the same experience.

Walter "Wolfman" Washington was finishing up his final set of the night. I saw Caroline in the bar mirror walking from the dance floor back to where I sat at the bar. She had her hair pulled back at her neck. She stopped next to my chair, rested her back against the bar and fanned herself with one of her hands. Perspiration beaded on her neck and the collar of her blue cotton dress was wet. She reached over and grabbed my glass of gin. With two fingers she delicately lifted out an ice cube and then, holding it in the palm of her hand, ran it across her forehead and then on her neck. To others it may have seemed like an act of sensuality. But to me it left no such impression.

"Alright," she said, as she held up the ice cube to ask with a gesture if I wanted what was left to be returned to my glass. I shook my head no. "Alright," she repeated, dropping the ice on the bar top. "Are you ready to hear my quotation for the night?" I remained silent for a few seconds. I could not physically drink any more alcohol. I was lightheaded and that familiar dryness was in my mouth. I knew that I was drunk. Caroline adjusted the ribbon with which she had tied her hair back and continued to look directly at me. She waited for me to respond to her. I nodded slowly without speaking and lifted my glass of gin and swallowed.

Caroline quickly reached her hand into a large pocket near the hip of her dress. She pulled out a piece of damp loose leaf paper which had been folded several times. She continued to look directly at me carefully, assessing, as she unfolded the paper. I heard a police siren in the distant New Orleans night.

"The reason I picked this quotation is because of a conversation we recently had. You'll remember," she said, overemphasizing her syllables, as if she knew I might be having trouble understanding her. "This quotation comes from Thornton Wilder's book entitled *The Bridge of San Luis Rey*," she then said. While I recognized Wilder's name, I could not remember any books I had ever read by him. "In the book," Caroline began to explain, "there is a point where the mother has the dreadful realization that her only daughter does not love her. Wilder is describing the effect that this realization has on the mother." Caroline paused to assure that I was listening. She looked at me and waited for an acknowledgment. I nodded again slightly. Caroline then lifted the loose-leaf page and read:

*The knowledge that she would never be loved in return
acted upon her ideas as a tide acts upon cliffs. Her religious beliefs went first... Next she lost her belief in the
sincerity of those about her...*

Caroline had read the paragraph slowly. Her voice seemed
to echo in my ears as the band ended its set. I found it hard to
focus on what she had said. In a matter of moments, the words
of the quote were shuffled and then lost to my memory. I stared
off, away from Caroline, trying to bring it back. Caroline folded
the page up and placed it in her pocket.

"When we talked about the possible relationship between
an abused childhood and your lack of belief in God, I was
unsure how to support the idea," she said. Caroline leaned
toward me and lowered her voice, in recognition that the band
had stopped playing. "This quotation made me think that
maybe it is not the abused childhood per se, but the feeling
of not being loved as a child by your parents that leads to
non-belief in God." She paused and looked at me. My head was
leaning forward slightly. She grabbed my hands and squeezed
them gently. I did not immediately respond, but lifted my head,
smiled, and looked briefly again at my image in the mirror
behind the bar. I had drunk too much to respond in any coher-
ent fashion. Caroline must have sensed this and turned away
from me to try and get the bartender's attention. "One coffee,"
I heard her say to Emily, the bartender.

FIFTEEN

~

Would you like to dance?" the woman asked, loudly, as if she wanted everyone present to hear the request. We were seated at a small table in the corner at a club called the Carrollton Station. It was one of those nights when I had avoided the Maple Leaf in protest over the tourists and the cover charge. As a result, Caroline had met me at the Carrollton Station several blocks from the Maple Leaf.

This should be interesting. I watched as Caroline's face reflected her struggling with her response. I thought, perhaps, I should intervene, play her boyfriend, and rescue her. Slowly, Caroline turned to face the woman and returned a smile, albeit uncomfortably.

"No, thank you."

The woman who had asked Caroline to dance placed an unlit cigarette in her mouth, with her head cocked back as if she was not sure how to smoke it, while staring at Caroline, and then moved brusquely away from our table without speaking further. Caroline's eyes followed the woman and then, covering her cheeks with her hands, she leaned across the table.

"I didn't know what to say," she said, in a grade school classroom whisper. I knew her well enough to know that she was blushing, even though I could not see it in the semi-darkness.

I gathered from what I knew of Caroline that her experience with lesbians was limited. I did not know whether her religious beliefs would impact her assessment of gay individuals. Despite my southern upbringing and its stereotypical elements, I had never felt threatened by homosexuals. Indeed, while my father periodically expressed racist sentiments when I was growing up I don't remember him ever saying anything derogatory about homosexuals. Caroline turned and looked in the direction in which the woman had walked away. I looked over, casually, as well. The woman was now standing at the bar with three or four other women, all of whom appeared to my untrained eyes to be gay. Unlike the woman who approached Caroline, the other women all had closely cut hair and were of stocky build. As Caroline continued to look, I interrupted her thoughts.

"If you keep staring at her, she may come back over here," I said, placing my hand on Caroline's arm for a moment. Caroline turned and looked at me as the band began a new song.

"Do you think I should have said 'yes'?" she asked.

I laughed aloud at Caroline's desire not to hurt someone's feelings. I knew her well enough to know that the sentiment she expressed was genuine. I reached across the table again and squeezed her hands. The music was too loud to talk further, but I looked at her with a reassuring wink.

"It's just a dance," I replied softly, not sure she heard me.

I then glanced back at the woman, who was in my line of sight. She was dancing by herself a few feet from her friends. She had a purple or red bandanna tied around her black shoulder length hair. There was a small thin braid of hair running down the back of her head. She leaned her head back as if staring at the ceiling and, while dancing, blew smoke rings upward.

Then, abruptly, the woman lowered her head and stopped dancing. Her back was toward us. She took a long slow drag on her cigarette. Her stillness stood in contrast to the motions of her friends who were now dancing with their hands in the air, a New Orleans second line, in a semicircle.

I watched as the woman turned, with apparent determination, and started walking toward our table. I knew that Caroline could not see the woman approaching our table. I thought it was best to warn Caroline of the woman's approach and caught Caroline's attention pointing with a finger on my hand that lay on the table. She glanced down at my hand. I assumed that she understood.

The woman arrived next to our table just as the band was finishing its song. She stood without speaking, at arm's length, hovering, as if lost in thought, or struggling to make a decision. I tried to restrain a grin as I wondered how Caroline would respond to another dance request.

"Do you mind if I ask your boyfriend to dance?" the woman, leaning over, asked Caroline. Caroline smiled widely with obvious enjoyment.

"No, I don't. 'It's just a dance' and he loves to dance," she said, throwing my words, she had in fact heard, back at me. The woman turned towards me. She had placed her cigarette back in her mouth. I thought it was not an unattractive mouth. I looked at Caroline and saw the laughter in her eyes. The band began another song. Without speaking, I started to stand up.

"Oh, it's a slow song," the woman said suddenly, with the cigarette still in the corner of her mouth. She looked away from me to the band as I stood there, jilted, unrequited, not knowing whether to respond. "I'll come back for a fast one," she said to Caroline, and then turned and without saying a word to me, quickly walked back toward the bar and her friends.

Caroline laughed while I remained standing. I raised my hands in the air, palms up, in mocked bewilderment.

"I guess she's bisexual," Caroline then stated matter-of-factly, before leaning forward and smiling into her hands.

As I lowered myself to sit, I replied, a bit unsure, that perhaps the woman just liked to dance. My strong sense, however, was that the woman was not the least interested in me, except for the express purpose of dancing. I had the unusual sense of feeling like an object. I recalled distantly, the oddness of that feeling from my days as a bartender, where you were quasi-famous merely because of the wooden bar you stood behind. In particular, I recalled two female backup singers in a band passing through town, and playing at the bar, who targeted me to sleep with. After my initial male enthusiasm, somewhere in the process, it all felt contrived. It was a sentiment which was supposed to be alien to the male ego that had been shaped in me.

After a few more drinks Caroline got up and began to dance with a younger fellow with a beard. The effect of the alcohol I had drank, and sitting alone, made me contemplate seeking out the gay woman to dance. While I scanned the room in a half-hearted attempt to find her, she promptly appeared beside me. She was standing on the edge of the dance floor with her hands folded together at her waist. She was looking out over the dance floor at Caroline. I watched her intensely as she stood there, but she never returned my gaze.

Her name was Loretta. She had recently finished her Ph.D. in clinical psychology and was in the process of setting up her practice. She eventually joined us at the table after one dance to a fast song with me. Actually, she danced by herself and used my presence as cover to do so. Once seated on Caroline's side of the table, she directed her conversation exclusively toward Caroline. It would have been easy for me to assume that her ignoring me was based simply on her sexual preference. Indeed, that reason might have set better with my vanity, if

I had been worried about it. However, again, my instincts were uncomfortable with such an easily derived conclusion. It seemed to me that something else was being played out in front of me. I kept quiet and tried to simply observe their interaction.

Loretta spoke to Caroline in an animated fashion. When Caroline responded to something Loretta said, she listened attentively. There was a tenderness and respect that she conveyed in her dealings with Caroline that would have seemed much more fitting if Caroline had been much older than Loretta.

Caroline appeared to be aware of this treatment, but I could not tell if she was uncomfortable with it, or with Loretta's presence.

Caroline, in response to a question from Loretta about employment, indicated that she was a grade school teacher on her summer break and then volunteered that I was a lawyer. Loretta glanced at me again. I sensed that she viewed me with a mixture of apprehension and disdain. I contemplated excusing myself, but felt Caroline would have never forgiven me had I left her alone with Loretta.

As the music continued to play, I noticed that Caroline was referring to me again. It appeared that she was trying to get me involved in the conversation. I leaned in to listen more closely and I heard Caroline, in response to Loretta indicating she had done her dissertation on an issue related to family secrets, telling Loretta that I had a difficult childhood.

"Ask away," I said, in response, interrupting Loretta's comments to Caroline about the possible effects of an abused childhood. As soon as I made the remark Loretta stopped speaking. There was an uncomfortable pause and then Loretta changed the topic. Loretta left with her friends shortly thereafter and Caroline and I did as well. Rebekah was getting back in town and I wanted to get home, mostly sober, to be there.

SIXTEEN

~

I watched Rebekah as she lay sleeping next to me. I noticed the short blonde hairs that grew at the base of her neck, seemingly unconnected with the rest of the hair on her head and I thought how similar these hairs looked to the first soft woolly blonde hairs of a young child. Even though it was 8:00 a.m. Rebekah was still sleeping soundly. Rebekah's most recent flight had not returned her to town until nearly midnight and it had taken her awhile to unwind and fall asleep. The sun shined strongly through the window blinds and light lay upon her face as I lay motionless in the bed next to her in silent contemplation.

I began to wonder what I had gotten myself into with Rebekah. Now that we had been living together for nine months, I felt there was something lacking. It was sometimes just a flat feeling and other times a dull ache in my stomach that warned me. My immediate thought, however pedantic, was that she was just not intellectual enough for me. I knew that she was intelligent. I guess I just felt she lacked any intellectual curiosity. Perhaps it was just that she did not share my intellectual intensity. But was that just an excuse for some deeper discomfort in me which I did not understand? She was comfortably complacent with an almost irrational non-reflective faith about life. On the other hand, I wanted to live and think passionately. In my mind, this put me in constant conflict with the world around me, which seemed staid and common, communistic in its rejection of the intellect. I longed for a more intellectually engaged life, although I lived my life in a state of permanent rebellion, turmoil, and occasional moments of despair, masking my desire to be truly free. I wanted freedom from ritual, freedom from materialism, freedom from the everyday mindlessness. At least this is what I told myself, what I held onto as sacred and self-defining. Albert Camus, in his book *The Rebel*, had written that all rebellion, at its base, is just a search for an alternative order to the one being imposed. If he was correct, I could not yet see clearly the order which I sought in my life. Living as I did too often created unnecessary chaos in my world, but I seemed incapable of calming the white capped waters of that troublesome instinct.

I had tried on several occasions to explain to Rebekah my feelings on the difference between intelligence and intellect, and why it was important to me that she understand, but had never succeeded at convincing her of the distinction, or its importance. Maybe, for her, like many others, it simply did not matter. Richard Hofstadter, the historian, had made it clear that while intelligence was "an excellence of mind that is employed within a fairly narrow, immediate, and predictable range," intellect was the "critical, creative and contemplative side of mind." It "examines, ponders, wonders, theorizes, criticizes, imagines." I saw myself as being intellectual, odd considering my proletariat upbringing, but it was part of my personal definition; the narrative I had created to set me apart and keep others at arm's length.

I had gone so far as to ask her on several occasions to read Jacques Barzun's *The House of Intellect*, or Richard Hofstadter's *Anti-Intellectualism in American Life*, in the hope that these might help her understand the difference, and, perhaps more importantly, better understand this aspect of me.

She had promised to read one or the other, but had never removed either copy from my bookshelf. Her message, intended or unintentional, was that these were my issues not hers. I felt the sting of that apathetic wasp.

Perhaps it was not lack of intellect but the fact that she accepted her fate more readily than me that I found disquieting. There were very few things in my life that I did not overturn, tear apart, and examine, at least in an intellectual manner. I sometimes wondered if she was familiar with the Lord Tennyson quote, often mistakenly cited by my father as a Marine Corp axiom, that: "Ours is not to reason why, ours is but to do and die." Her approach to life seemed to mirror that maxim. She was, in many ways, my intellectual antithesis. I struggled with acceptance of who she was and the clash with my need for her approval.

Although the reasons for it were unclear to me I recognized that I had, what seemed, an inordinate need to feel that the people who were closest to me truly understood who I was and what I believed. For a long time I rationalized this need as a natural outgrowth of my desire to live passionately, and because, as an atheist creating my own system, I thought I lived without other societal moorings, or reference points. Instinctively, I unfairly tried to force my friends to be those familial reference points, the ballasts in my life, a role most did not want, and others, fighting their own discreet battles, were incapable of fulfilling. Now, in light of my discussions with Caroline, I wondered if it was simply the unfulfilled longing of my childhood to be loved and understood; the simple desire we all have to be part of a happy ending. I had read that both Nietzsche and Dostoevsky had struggled with similar unfulfilled needs. I wondered about the similarities in our childhoods and our belief systems.

In any event, I had the concern about Rebekah and our compatibility before she moved in with me. I was convinced, however, that I was in love and that these other things did not matter. I tried very hard to gloss over any potential negatives, to ignore that tell-tale warning pain in my gut; the guardian that protected me, even though my stomach was often a better judge than my intellect of my repressed emotions, of my need for flight. Now I wondered sometimes if I had not confused love with lust. I was not naive and I knew that, as to what love was, I was creating the definition on my own as I went along. I had no strong sense, no repositories of memories, of how it felt to be loved or to love someone. I understood duty. I understood discipline. These things, Marine Corp. duty and discipline, were my waking companions, my parental teachers, as a child. Anyway, to the best of my ability to understand the distinction between love and lust, I loved her. I never really thought about other women once we started going out and I still didn't. Wasn't that love? When we argued, I was always left with a feeling of dread if the matter wasn't resolved. Certainly that must be love. On occasion when I thought about ending the relationship and living on my own again, I would realize her importance in my life. Was that love?

For her part, and from my perspective, it seemed that it was so easy for her to love me. I was never quite sure why she did. I was genuinely hopeless at the minor day to day tasks that most people's lives revolved around. It was not because I was incapable of such things, but rather because I simply refused to do them, to be enslaved by them. I found compliance with these desensitized and socialized rituals demeaning, refused to be compliant, and I cast a broad net in my ethical discontent. For example, I refused to honor birthdates, or other holidays, with gifts because I did not like being told when or what I was supposed to celebrate. I rejected the capitalist marketing

impulse inherent in such celebrations, and the need for constant mind-numbing distraction, which I felt was behind it.

I hardly ever went shopping for anything other than an
occasional suit for work, groceries and liquor. The capitalist
system, I often thought, would collapse, or shrink drastically,
if it had to depend on me. My non-work clothes were generally
all second hand, mostly given to me by old girlfriends who, at
various times in my life, had practiced their maternal instincts
on me. On rare occasions, I would go to the Salvation Army
if I needed a specialty item like a sweat shirt. My fashion in
clothes was a confusing mix between what I needed to play
lawyer and a "style," if you will, developed when I was living
on $300.00 per month as a student. As my dear friend, Gautier,
the writer, humorously put it, I was a "fashion anarchist." I was
proud of the fact that I could not name the designer of a single
suit, tie or dress shirt. It was my own way of refusing to allow
my life to be concerned about such things, or to be governed
by the materialistic commercialization of society. I refused to
inoculate the emotional and intellectual needs we all have with
such illusory antidotes.

My entire wardrobe, other than clothes for work, consisted
of five or six T-shirts, three pairs of blue jeans, a half dozen
pair of boxer shorts and some old red high-top Converse tennis
shoes. For some reason, I did have lots of socks.

Rebekah put up with my disrespect for fashion, although I
never believed, despite my attempts to explain, that she understood its genesis. She would occasionally suggest that I might
want to discard an old T-shirt, but she never got pushy about
it and she never, on her own volition, tossed out any of my
clothes. She would neatly fold my T-shirts with several holes
after washing and with a gentle prod, which I would ignore,
might say that a particular shirt had "seen better days."

In contrast, Rebekah owned lots of clothes. She knew all the clothing designers' names and would tell me she had bought a "such and such" dress, as if the fact that she had purchased a dress by this particular designer added meaning to her life. She had at least 40 or 50 dresses as well as accompanying scarves, jewelry, hats and scores of shoes, hose, brassieres, blouses, and slacks. Mysteriously, though, she always said that she had "nothing to wear." My befuddlement at the phrase had no wryness; it was simply as if she was saying "we have no dishes" while we were stacking dishes. There was apparently a language in which these things made sense, but it was a language to which I was not privy. It was as if my language was too literal and hers was more like atonal jazz, or some developing aspect of physics, where there could be many things and nothing in her closet at the same time. To her credit, after moving in with me, she also bought a few simple cotton dresses. She knew I liked the cotton dresses the best and she would often wear these on the weekends when we went out together.

I had not made things easy on her in other regards. I had lived without a phone for most of my adult life, but she had to have one so photographers and her agent could contact her. Although I compromised and agreed to let her get one for the house, I generally refused to answer the phone at any time, or talk to anyone on it.

My refusal to have a phone had its roots in those years when, as a student, I simply could not afford one. That initial decision, based on lack of funds, morphed into a principled one over time. Our ethics are too often determined by our circumstances. I decided that not having a phone eliminated the nonessential communication in my life. Someone might call on the phone to chat about some frivolous topic, but they were not likely to get in their car and drive over to my house to do it. Maybe it insulated me in other ways that I did not realize.

I had also never owned a television. Rebekah had two in her apartment when we met, one for her living room and one for her bedroom. Both televisions were color, but I refused to allow color TV in my house based on nothing more than the vague principle that TV was invented in black and white. It was perfectly symbolic of my ill-defined revolt against the entire world around me. I had to work in that world and was bound by the social contract, which I often said was made without my consent, but I did not have to allow my life to revolve around the mindless "things" that people grasped onto to fill their time.

I ultimately compromised and permitted her to bring into the house a very old black and white tube television that she found at a garage sale. I remember the look on her face when she arrived at the house after buying it for $10. She already knew, without asking, that I would accept it as a compromise.

The television took three to four minutes to warm up and I expected it to go out at any moment, but it kept playing. After a while, I developed a grudging admiration of the old TV and on occasion, I would watch The Three Stooges on it. For all the issues I wrestled with I could still be a child and watch the Three Stooges alone and laugh out loud.

Rebekah also wanted badly to marry me, but I would not consent. I saw no purpose to marriage and felt certain, with more women working and leaving the home defeating the economic justification, it would fade away as an institution, like organized religion, over time. On one night, however, after two bottles of wine and prolonged sex, we agreed to split a set of earrings she had purchased. Naked, covered in sweat, and seated on the floor of the living room, with empty wine bottles as our attending audience, we exchanged earrings in a private wedding ceremony. It was the closest we would ever feel to each other.

SEVENTEEN

~

I finished off my third gin and tonic and motioned to Emily the bartender for another. As I set the glass down, my head was heavy with facts. I had spent the better part of the afternoon meeting with two female friends who were interested in learning what rights they might have to claim sexual harassment against a male co-worker. I was surprised to learn that the male co-worker, Richard, was a guy whom I knew through a former girlfriend. I did not know Richard very well, but I still saw him occasionally at The Maple Leaf.

The recent television hearings on Clarence Thomas' Supreme Court nomination were still vivid in Susan and Claudia's minds at our meeting. I recalled the hearings and my disgust with the circus atmosphere of it all. I also recalled reading the news reports and the disappointment over the affair as it distracted from the very real possibility that I thought the Thomas hearings could produce, namely that the black community would no longer be presented by the media as a political monolith. The possibility of debate between blacks over substantive political and ethical issues was lost. It was back to stereotypes and simplistic thinking for white America. I had not cared whether Thomas was nominated prior to the Anita Hill hearings, but I was optimistic that it would be a positive process for the black and white communities. The hearing derailed that brief optimism.

It had turned out that Susan and Claudia were being sub-
jected to what appeared to be a form of sexual harassment
known as hostile environment. Richard had made a habit of
telling sexual jokes and making sexual comments at work. In
the meeting, both Susan and Claudia detailed the jokes that
were told in their presence. As I listened, I recognized the jokes
as ones that I had heard from a client or two. I also realized
that I had repeated several of these jokes to male friends or
clients. I gave Susan and Claudia advice on their rights but
declined the possible representation.

As I was waiting for my drink, with the palms of my hands
flat on the bar, I became aware that someone had sat down
next to me. I turned to see the outline of a face that was somewhat familiar to me.

"Where is your friend, Caroline?" the voice said. I tried
focusing on the woman's facial features and did not immediately respond to her. "I'm Loretta," she said, somewhat flus-
tered, and apparently sensing that I did not recognize her.
After a further pause with no response from me, and in a more
demanding tone, she repeated, "Where is Caroline?"

"I don't know," I finally replied, as I lifted the glass Emily
had just placed in front of me. I took a long sip and watched
Emily walk away. Loretta looked over her shoulder toward the
entrance of the bar as if to check to see whether someone she
was expecting had just walked in. She then set her drink on
the bar and sat quietly. I knew, unfortunately, that the quiet
would not last. I was drawn inward and my quiet was a way of
recharging myself. I needed to be still and alone. I closed my
eyes for a moment and tried to meditate and think of nothing.

"By the way . . . is she gay?" Loretta then asked awkwardly.
I heard her ask that question, but picked up my glass and I
swallowed some gin before answering. Loretta became impa-
tient and breathed angrily through her mouth waiting for my

reply. I heard the strains of Jimi Hendrix playing Dylan's "All Along the Watchtower" from the jukebox and let it wash over me. I wanted to return to my quiet, but found I could not.

"I think you confuse sincerity with sexual preference," I replied dryly, without looking at Loretta. "She is not gay," I then said, with perhaps too much emphasis on the word "not." Loretta started to fidget on her barstool.

"Well, everyone is part gay," she then said, in a matter of fact, lecturing, tone. I was not sure whether the comment was an invitation to debate but, regardless, I did not feel like participating. I had a sudden surge of my growing misdirected hostility.

"Maybe in your world, sweetheart," I replied, turning aggressively toward Loretta. She seemed unsure, but then regained her composure.

"Well, aren't we tough," Loretta said, sarcastically, as she started to pick up her drink and get off of her barstool.

"Blow me," I replied, in a condescending tone. I turned away from her and lifted my glass to drink.

Loretta walked away from the bar without further comment. I stared hard at my drink which now rested between both of my hands on the bar. I felt the coolness of the damp glass on my skin. I was immediately concerned about my comments to Loretta.

It was always uncomfortable to me when I exhibited hostility of any type, which was occurring now, without explanation, more frequently. Why? Others might claim that anger was a normal emotion. For me, however, it was not and I fought to stop any such display. I had contained it, remained aloof from it, for most of my life. But recently I was too often losing the battle, being periodically overtaken by it, and getting angry over silly things; projecting some inner anger with myself on to others, unsuspecting. Somewhere locked in my head, behind whatever un-scaled protective walls I had built, there was a link between my fear of anger and my childhood. I knew it existed, but I had never been able to find the right key to that lock, so that I could explore it more completely.

When I was a young teenager, and still small, my father, a former Marine who said he had been in many fights, repeatedly lectured me that when I could not avoid a fist fight I should always throw the first punch and, he insisted, throw it as hard as you could. "You may lose the fight, but its important that the other guy know he has been in a fight," he said. His admonition to his undersized less hateful son was for future fist fights, like those in his own youth, that he envisioned for me. I began to feel that, perhaps, I internalized the advice for other aspects of my life: hit first, hurl the first insult, knock the other person back on their heels, before they could hurt me. It had created a neural pathway in my brain that became habitual.

I sat quietly again. I collected myself to calm the rising anger with an image that I often used at night to put myself to sleep. I closed my eyes, blocked out the sounds around me, and thought of the Mogollon people's cliff dwellings in the Gila National Forest in New Mexico. I thought of the isolation of those high dwellings, imagined the layout of the cave walls within the mountain and the fact that the only possible approaches were in front of them. I saw the short walls inside the caves. I recalled sitting there two years earlier with my friend Holly and marveling at the fact that nothing could approach, or threaten, the Mogollon people without being seen; it was a built-in security measure to keep its inhabitants from potential harm. And I tried to take myself back to sitting on the carved stone lip of those ancient dwellings. The world was filled with my immediate anger, but I had the cliff dwellings. It gradually calmed me. It always did.

EIGHTEEN

~

W hat's bothering you?" Rebekah asked the next morning, standing with her back to the old black and white television. I was looking for my car keys under the cushions on the sofa and turned toward her. My stomach hurt. Somewhere at the edges of my consciousness, that I sought to retreat from, I knew my apparent indifference was hurting her.

"I am going to drive over to the library to do some more research before it closes," I told her, dryly, ignoring her larger question, as folks in relationships too often do.

"But is something wrong?" she asked, with an increasing frustration, knowing already that I would be unable to answer her question.

I lifted my hands, palms up, and shrugged my shoulders a bit like a confused and inarticulate child. The process in my brain that formed sentences was inordinately slowed. Sometimes, briefly, it ceased completely and I had no words to express myself. At such time language and expression seemed difficult for me.

"I'm not really sure," I finally replied, without making eye contact. When I responded in that fashion, it was all I was capable of saying. No other words formed in my mind as I stood there waiting for the words of a sentence to coalesce. Whenever I got angry I inevitably shut down. It was as if I was preparing myself for the beating I assumed would follow.

My mood was too often changing without me being aware of the cause for the change. However, within a few minutes, and through careful and continued prodding from Rebekah, I realized that I was focusing my conversation on two issues: namely my unease over the sexual harassment allegations of Claudia and Susan and my bigger concern over having told Loretta off.

"You have never responded very well whenever you have gotten angry with anyone," Rebekah stated, in a self-assured tone. Her response reflected the thoughts of someone who has studiously observed the habits of their spouse, or lover, for many years. I recognized in it her ability to empathize. But I was surprised that she had noticed this particular characteristic of mine, which had taken me years to recognize.

I recalled my adolescence as a time when I tried very hard to control any anger I felt. The reasons for implementing that control were lost to my memory. At some point, I apparently internalized my anger, hypnotized it away, and for many years it rarely manifested itself. I assumed my more recent despondence was over my growing inability to keep the anger under control. Perhaps there was a larger issue involved. I was vaguely aware that I carried an image of me as an out-of-control child, a failure. I wasn't sure if it was my own image of me, or an ingrained image impressed upon me by parents during my childhood. Or maybe I feared that I had the genetic chip of my father and his father in me that would lead me to harm others.

"You know, it's alright for you to express anger on occasion," she said to me, as she continued to stand in front of the television. I motioned softly for her to come sit next to me on the sofa. "And you should not suppress it. Just acknowledge it and let it pass. If you suppress it, it comes out sideways."

"I guess I don't like to lose control," I replied, in a self-defeating tone, as she sat down.

"I think that's an understatement," she replied. I did not respond, but I was not offended by the remark. My thought process was slowly reconnecting, through her attentiveness.

"I think you need to understand that there is a difference between anger and rage," she finally said, breaking the silence between us. "It's really rage, which you equate with your childhood, that you are afraid of. There is nothing wrong with becoming angry," she said, fidgeting a bit and placing her other hand on my arm. "Look, you were familiar with rage growing up and it scares you," she said. "It scares you because you fear that you are capable of doing to others what others did to you as a child," she continued. "But I know you. You can be difficult, but you are not mean. And you do not carry your father's anger. You are just not one who suffers fools easily."

Again I did not respond immediately, but simply pursed my lips as I felt unfamiliar emotions welling up. I was still feeling a bit dull and at times like these, when despondency over my anger overtook me, it was almost as if my mind purposely ceased to comprehend. It shut me down to avoid the pain. Thinking became harder. I had never thought much about the possible distinction between anger and rage. I was, however, familiar, in a vague way, with my fear that I possessed the same abusive traits that were visited upon me when I was young. I was my father as he was his father.

"It is okay for you to show your emotions, even if it's anger you are showing," she said, as she stood up. "It's just amazing you have controlled them this long. Just let go and you'll find nobody will think any less of you," she said. Rebekah then moved about the room. Maybe I thought. But I would think less of me. Would my anger prove the worst things said of me as a child? I didn't know and had no way of knowing absent a full-blown meltdown, which I was not going to let happen. I was still a puzzle to myself with missing emotional pieces. I sat still for a few more seconds slowly processing her words.

"And as far as the sexual harassment allegations," Rebekah suddenly continued, "don't carry it around like it's something you did. You are not responsible for every jerk in the world."

I again forced a smile on my face. Rebekah turned and began to leave the room. How could she see so far into me I wondered, this woman whom I too often thought was not intellectual enough. Was that love? After sitting for a minute or so, and letting her comments sink in, I continued my search for my keys.

NINETEEN

~

I prayed today that God will cause you to believe in Him," she said to me, in a purposely uplifting tone. I watched the band setting up on the stage. The jukebox started playing the next song and within a few notes I immediately recognized the deep organ strains of a gospel tune---*This may be the last time*--by The Blind Boys of Alabama.

Perhaps because I had drunk a few gin and tonics before she showed up, I found the comment ridiculous. I had been taking depositions all day, slaying the consuming dragon of work and I had not put down the sword yet, so my mind was still programmed for immediate responses and prompt follow-up questions. I set my drink down and exhaled heavily.

"Caroline, come on. That is such bullshit," I finally replied. She looked at me a bit concerned. I ignored the look.

"I can pray for you if I choose," Caroline then replied sternly. She was not intimidated, never was intimidated by me.

"There is no logic in your prayer," I responded, in an overly animated fashion, gesturing with my hands, because of the alcohol in me. She hesitated.

"Why do you say that?"

"Your prayer is based on the assumption that your God could make me believe in Him -- right?" I asked too abruptly. Caroline moved her glass of soda water in her hand before replying, searching for the trip wire on the intellectual trap I might be setting.

"Of course," she said, affirmatively, but still unsure.

"Well, if He does not have the power to make me believe, your prayers are fruitless, correct?" I asked tersely, as
the baritone voice of one of the Blind Boys continued in the
background.

"Alright," she answered less reluctantly. "I believe that He
has the power to make you believe in Him."

"Well, if He has the power to force me to believe, and save
myself, why hasn't He done so? If He has the power to save
me from eternal damnation and He does not do so, then He
is apathetic to my damnation, to my future. Or maybe He in-
tends it," I said, leaning forward slightly in my chair. Caroline
said nothing in response. She let my defense sit between us for
me to see it. Her bangs partially covered her forehead as she
looked away from me to the dance floor.

"And if He has such power and exercises it and makes
me believe, that also means that I have no free will," I said.
"Because I don't believe in God and, under your theory, have no
free will, since He can make me believe or not believe as He
chooses, my lack of belief in Him is caused by Him." I took in
a long breath. Caroline sat stoically, measuring me.

"So, don't waste your time praying to a God who is either
impotent to change, or apathetic at best, to my fate." I concluded my remarks with mild annoyance. I looked at Caroline
briefly and back into the mirror behind the bar. I felt anger
rising up in me. I am being absurd. Why the confrontation?
Where was this belligerence coming from? I lifted my glass and
noticed it was mostly ice. The bartender was occupied at the
other end of the bar. The jukebox went silent.

While I believed what I had said, I suddenly felt that
familiar remorse over the tone I had used. My hostility had
come forth from a place within that I could not identify and

was directed at my best friend. My emotions were coming out sideways, over things that should not have provoked them.

Caroline stood up as if to leave, but then moved to within inches of where I sat on my barstool. She leaned herself into me aggressively.

"If you are right and you have no free will then God causes your hostility toward God. God makes you hostile toward Himself or Herself. That conclusion is stupid!" she finally said, loud enough to be heard by others when she used the word 'stupid,' who must have assumed a drunken lovers' spat was taking place.

"Get a hotel room!" someone yelled out. Others laughed.

Caroline was annoyed. She asked me to look at her and, confrontationally, moved her face even closer to mine.

"Look at me," she demanded again, when I did not immediately reply. She pointed her finger at me as the jukebox started a Cajun waltz. "Sometimes your logic blinds you. It's a crutch for you not learning how to feel things. You need to unlearn your logic and learn to see with your heart," she said emphatically. She pulled her finger away from my face and poked me hard in the chest. She returned to her barstool and sat down. I sat without expression and looked into the mirror and not at her. What was I doing? She immediately stood back up.

"Tusa, if you are so big on *The Little Prince*, why is it that you haven't retained the basic lesson of the story?" she lectured. I had rarely seen Caroline this intense in our conversations. I contemplated not responding, but I could not back down from the argument. My whole life I had felt pushed and my natural instinct was to push back, even if I realized I was doing so for the wrong reasons, blindly. Unfortunately, I sometimes forgot any other form of interaction and my social relationships simply masked me pushing everyone around me until they tired of it and left me. She was a true friend to put up with me, and to challenge me.

"If your God exists and He gave me the ability to reason, it makes no sense to me that He would then expect me not to use the logic my reason shows me," I replied, trying to lower the temperature of the conversation.

"So what! If no God exists, how is it that you have any ability to reason?" Caroline asked, animated. She was sweating and I could see the perspiration on her neck. I noticed a large bulging vein that ran down the side of her small neck.

I had gotten control of my annoyance. The alcohol steadied me. I smiled at her and managed to let go of the tension I had felt. As soon as I made eye contact with her, her face softened and she sat back on her barstool. I leaned gently towards her.

"The ability to reason is clearly not proof of the existence or nonexistence of a God," I said, slightly above a whisper.

"That's BS and you know it," Caroline quickly interrupted, but not in as agitated tone as before. "We all have the ability to reason, why is it that we all have that ability, it has to be that some force has shaped us, made us, and given us the ability to reason," she said, placing her hands in her lap, and making a form of the theological argument by design. She looked at me intensely and, ironically, at that moment, as I pulled myself away from the ledge of my isolation, nearly drowning in my own unfocused anger, quarreling with her, I realized that she loved me. It was an unspoken aesthetic love. I sensed nothing sexual in its content and, for the first time in my life, for the very first time, knew that it was an unconditional love. It was a feeling I realized I had never experienced, the contours which, in a lifetime of seeking, were unfamiliar to me.

Freud had once written: "I cannot count on the love of many people. I have not pleased, comforted, edified them." This was something that somewhere in my life's progression, on an indeterminate date, I had internalized as part of my narrative, the story I told myself. Expect nothing from others and you won't be disappointed. Now I was blindsided, overturned, by the unwarranted gift I was receiving from Caroline.

I sat without speaking and the thought of her unconditional love, of someone actually directing that to me, of all people, who did not deserve it, overpowered me. Damn my intellect. The emotional impact, struggling as I was with other issues, overwhelmed me. Tears welled in my eyes and I feared that speaking would further unman me. In the distance, the soundtrack of the first feelings of unconditional love, Bob Dylan sang the haunting end chorus of *Just Like a Woman*: "but she breaks just like a little girl," on the jukebox. I breathed in and as I blinked felt a tear run down my cheek. Caroline saw it, reached over and placing her hand on my face, wiped the tear away with her thumb. Did she know what I was feeling? I exhaled slowly.

"I don't concede that we all have the ability to reason," I said, my words breaking up slightly by an uncontrolled emotion, while still leaning toward her. "But your argument is a circle. You cannot prove that the existence of a God is a prerequisite to my ability, or all of our abilities to reason. It does not appear to me to be a prerequisite any more than the fact that we all have ears means there is a God. Commonality means nothing. I have skin, a fish has scales, does this difference mean there is no God?" I asked rhetorically, and as my voice strengthened.

Caroline suddenly laughed. It was a school girl's giggle that lifted me and preceded her lightly slapping her thigh with her hand. Her mood changed as she apparently thought about my comparison. I straightened up, smiled myself, as a last tear formed, and raised my glass again to indicate to the bartender, who had looked my way, that I needed a refill.

"Sometimes I think you would be a better fish than a Christian," Caroline said, smiling widely, supportively, at me. There was a hint of resignation in her voice, but she still smiled. I looked back at her.

"Fortunately, I am neither," I replied, more composed.

"No," she responded. "You are a Christian, you just don't yet believe in God." She emphasized the word "yet" as she spoke.

The jukebox began playing another song. I soon recognized Steve Marriot's distinctive vocals on Humble Pie's *30 Days in the Hole*. Caroline turned away for a moment to speak briefly with the woman seated on the other side of her. The song took me back to a night in 1972 at the Warehouse on the corner of Tchoupitoulas and Felicity street. We had squeezed through the entrance and made our way to the bleachers. I could feel the heat and perspiration of that evening. I was momentarily back at the Warehouse, my favorite venue for seeing music in the early 70's, listening to Humble Pie. I felt safe, lighter, bolstered by the thought of an unconditional love I did not understand and which I was incapable of reciprocating. It did not matter whether there was or was not a God. It did not matter whether Caroline prayed for me. For 30 seconds the thought of her unconditional love and a long ago concert freed me.

TWENTY

~

I did not see her approach me. When I did realize that she was next to me, she was leaning toward me, familiar, and kissing me on the cheek. I turned to see the mischievous smile that had once enchanted me, and that I remembered so well, with her dimples up high on the side of each freckled cheek. Her brown-red hair was pulled back lazily, incompletely, by a rubber band near the base of her neck. The small scar above her right eyebrow was still there, but had broadened by time and dulled in appearance since I had last seen her. But her eyes, large and green, still drew me to her. The time that had passed made us older, more worn and distracted, beaten down in too many ways, but her eyes still blazed with the unbridled intensity I recalled from our college days. I glanced down and noticed that her left hand was being held by a slightly distressed four year old child who was a darker image of her mother. This was obviously her daughter Nesta. The little girl was the product of a two-week relationship with a Jamaican bass player in a reggae band and, hence, she was given the moniker of reggae's greatest artist, Bob "Nesta" Marley. Where she and I had once lived, like most twenty year olds of our generation, without any real notion of the future, time was now gradually and firmly holding us in its grasp through a child.

"Well," Annabelle said. I snapped back to the reality of the moment.

"This must be Nesta," I said, bending over a bit and placing my hand on the child's head, as if it was the appropriate social thing to do. Nesta did not answer and, in fact, hardly paid any attention to me. She simply looked around the airport with that "young child in distress" look, but she did not cry. I turned and hugged Annabelle. No words were exchanged between us. It was easy to feel comfortable around her. Long ago lovers and old friends sometimes do not need new language between them to define and thereby restrict. Annabelle was my singular memory of acceptance explored, prior to Caroline. Maybe, in the end, and as we age, and passion and physicality diminish, that's all love really is, acceptance of the other.

We headed down toward the airport lobby to retrieve Annabelle and Nesta's luggage. They were in town from Austin, Texas for the wedding of Annabelle's college roommate, Debbie, who was also almost the mother of my child. I had agreed to pick them up at the airport.

Debbie, long before she met the doctor she was about to marry, had decided that she needed to be "with child." As she explained to Annabelle and me over too many drinks one night at The Continental Club in Austin, the biological clock which her mother had drilled into her psyche, even in her twenties, was running faster. As I had known her since high school, she had decided that I would be a good donor for her experiment. Annabelle, who I was dating at the time, thought it all sounded fine. Debbie promised Annabelle she could be the godmother. They decided that night that the child would be baptized in the Catholic Church, even though neither was Catholic, because they liked the stained glass windows in the big Catholic Church up the street from Annabelle's house.

Having never wanted children I found the prospect daunting. I always feared that I would be a poor father and had decided early in life that it would be better to wake up at 65 years old wishing I had children than to wake up finding out that I had become my father or his father. I pleaded for more time to think about her proposal.

Debbie made it clear, as we talked that night, that she was only interested in my chromosomes. Annabelle and Debbie discussed openly, as if I was not present, that they would have to institute several environmental changes so the child would not end up like me. I actually thought seriously about her offer to be a father for several days. Even though I was not raised to worry about biological clocks and had never expressed a desire to have kids, I found myself, after she asked if I would consider it, mulling over the offer and its ramifications. Fortunately, or unfortunately, for me and the Darwinian descent of my genes, before I could respond to the offer, Debbie got drunk several nights later and slept with some high school dropout named Bill. She had let a scrub bull into the registered cow's barn yard. Timing is everything in life and my hesitation, her genetic clock, and the currency of our youth, gave Bill his chance.

My daydreaming about my missed fatherhood was interrupted when we reached the escalators that went down to the baggage section of the New Orleans airport. Nesta refused to set foot on the escalator. She looked at the moving metal steps the way a mechanic looks at a set of written instructions he has to review in order to fix a car engine, after unsuccessful attempts to fix it without the instructions. Nesta crinkled her eyebrows down, turned her lips down, crossed her arms and shook her head emphatically 'no.' Annabelle had no luck convincing Nesta to take the escalator and Nesta refused to be carried down. As a result, we walked over to the stairs on the other side of the lobby.

After retrieving their luggage, we all went to my car and put the luggage in the trunk. Nesta's personality took over again and she insisted that we drive with all the windows down. We left the airport with the wind blowing in the car and Nesta hanging out the window, while standing in Annabelle's lap, the way dogs do to try and taste or smell the breeze.

Annabelle and I talked a little during the drive, but it was mostly surface chatter like how Nesta had been doing and how work was going. It was in stark contrast to the conversations we had often had years ago when we danced around the issue of whether we were "in love," and what "love" meant and required of us. In those days, we would sit, in the early morning, yogi style, under the pecan tree at her house, shelling pecans that the tree had generously dropped and drinking orange juice or hot tea. We would discuss her developing theory on the relationship between capitalism and marriage. She had a deft and nimble mind. In a strange sense, she lived above and below the common man, never experiencing his struggles, or feeling the gravity of his fears, while simultaneously laughing at the egos of all men.

"Men are so easy to manipulate," she had said, in a voice of experience, that I found easy to believe.

"And me?" I recall asking, unsure, but trying to be aloof, as if her answer did not concern me.

"Working on it. You're harder to unpack," she replied.

"Thanks for the warning. I'll try to be more difficult," I replied.

"You already are," she said.

We were inseparable then. My open defiance against the world around me was matched and supported by her stronger anarchic spirit which never seemed to damper. She openly attacked those who challenged me on my beliefs, once referring to a barroom combatant as a "needle dick bug fucker." And then she left to hitchhike in Europe with a mutual friend and I moved back to New Orleans.

Now, and for the last three years, she was living in Fort Collins, Colorado with a professor of physics at Colorado State. We had rarely conversed or written during the last few years. Every so often I would get a card or a picture of Nesta from her. It seemed to me that she had become a mild caricature of her philosophical self from years back, hemmed in, perhaps, by the duties of parenthood. In a sense we all had done so as we got older and jettisoned the heavier baggage of our experimental youth. If you are not careful in life you become exactly what you rebelled against. Society, with the grace and efficiency of Chinese water torture, wears down our edges and gets its way with most of us sooner or later.

Her only concerns now were related to Nesta and, marginally, the professor. Still, the image of her that stayed with me was of the pecan eating orange juice drinking anarchist who referred to housewives as "house plants" and thought that marriage was a dehumanizing economic arrangement and legalized prostitution a more humane approach to getting screwed for economics.

"At least the prostitute knows what she's doing and has the candor to admit it," she would say, in those heroic days.

I wondered what she would think about all that now. I decided it was better to preserve what remained of that more pleasing image in my head and not ask. I was certainly in no position to be critical. My rebellion had left me, as Allen Ginsberg wrote in *Howl*, with alarm clocks falling on my head every morning.

Our metaphysical rebellion was worthwhile because it shaped something deep inside of us. It was borne of things we did not understand and it drove us to experience great extremes. It gave life, without a God, some sense of temporal meaning. But ultimately was it significant? I looked over at Annabelle and she returned my gaze. A prior uninhibited lifetime passed between us in that glance.

I dropped off Annabelle and Nesta at their hotel. I had halfheartedly offered that they could stay with me and Rebekah, but Annabelle, perhaps sensing my lack of enthusiasm for having a four-year-old in the house, declined. She kissed me after I took her luggage out of the car.

"I'll talk to you before the wedding, I'm sure. A wedding! How ridiculous," she said. I watched her walk away holding Nesta's hand and allowed myself to wonder "what if" for a moment. Would our lives have been any different had we stayed together? Could her spirit have helped me shape a better vision of my/our future, or would the inevitable compromises hoisted on one or both of us have made us bitter and driven a wedge between us? I stopped myself from thinking as I walked around to get back in the car. Sometimes it's just nice to have stood on Mount Nebo and glimpsed the unattainable, and hold it in time. We had held the world at bay, briefly, and I would declare my victory on that point and go home.

TWENTY-ONE

~

I set down my book of poems by Charles Bukowski on the coffee table. Bukowski was an easy and amusing read and his lack of a traditional poetic structure was comforting. I could feel some affiliation when I read Bukowski. I was not sure it was an entirely emotional response, just a sense of identity with his words and with his unvarnished view of the world. When he wrote that it was better to be driven around by a woman who owns a red Porsche than to own one yourself, I understood. When he wrote that there was a bluebird in his heart that he wouldn't let out, I felt his struggle and sensed a shared dismay with the world and oneself, a lost memory.

Rebekah had finished dressing and had walked into the living room. We were already a few minutes late to leave for the wedding.

I watched from the sofa as Rebekah sorted through her purse. She wore a simple white cotton dress with one of her shoulders exposed. As a creative touch, for me, she had taken an old blue table cloth with embroidered patterns and had it tied as a sash of sorts around her waist. I liked the simplicity of it. But honestly, in my mind, she was so naturally beautiful, she would have looked good wearing a garbage bag.

In contrast, I was wearing a black tuxedo. I had not worn a tuxedo since high school and the 1970's powder blue prom model. As I stood up, Rebekah turned and faced me. She adjusted my cummerbund down slightly so the middle of it was even with the top of my pants. She stepped back and looked me over. I stood uncomfortably still. I did not understand, or appreciate, rituals of any type and this was just one more. I would be happy as soon as I could take the tuxedo off. Rebekah must have sensed my uneasiness.

"You look wonderful," she said, with an easy girl-friend smile.

During the church services I sat with Rebekah near the front of the church. As I was not religious, I did not kneel down with everyone else, recite prayers, or otherwise partici-pate in the services. My refusal to kneel brought a few stares from those who did not know me. However, Rebekah per-formed all of the applicable rituals and I sensed her nearness to me probably eased the blow, to those observing, of my reli-gious nonconformity. It is often the case in social life that the male member of a couple benefits from the ritualistic social actions of the female member. Richer folks had formalized this arrangement with the husband working while the wife joins all the appropriate charitable organizations. But even at my end of the social ladder the paradigm appeared to still hold.

I listened to the priest say that Debbie and Frederick were a "wonderful couple" who were starting their life together. I wondered if the priest even knew them prior to the wedding arrangements. I knew the church had some pre-marriage con-ferences with those intending to marry. I also wondered what the Catholic Church's rules were about women who had chil-dren out of wedlock getting married. I looked several rows up and noticed Debbie's daughter, Samantha. The church pew was hard and I wondered how long the service would last.

After the church ceremony we drove to a large reception hall. Rebekah and I sat at a table where we were ultimately joined by Annabelle and Nesta. Nesta looked terribly unhappy in her pink ruffled dress. She kept pulling at her hair which

Annabelle had piled up in some fashion and pinned on the top of her head. I thought for a moment, as I watched, what it would be like to be responsible for a child. I still knew that I would be a terrible parent.

Rebekah knew that at one time Annabelle and I had dated. In fact, she knew, because I had told her, that I generally regarded Annabelle as my first love. Usually, Rebekah, confident in her own beauty and the competitiveness with other women, gave no impression of being jealous when I was around female friends. She certainly never expressed any form of jealousy about my friendship with Caroline.

I noticed, however, that Rebekah acted very cool toward Annabelle. When Annabelle tried to engage Rebekah in conversation, Rebekah would respond in a monotone voice and, it appeared, in as few words as possible. Annabelle seemed aware of the treatment and, true to that anarchic spirit I recalled, responded by simply ignoring Rebekah thereafter, and talking directly to me. This too seemed to be annoying Rebekah so to avoid any problems, I asked Rebekah to dance.

"Are you all right?" I asked her, as we settled into a slow waltz.

"Yes," Rebekah replied, following my dance lead.

"I'm not Annabelle. You can respond to me with more than one word." Rebekah put her head on my shoulder and then kissed me on the neck.

"I'm sorry," she said, as she lifted her head and held my head with her hands. "But there is something about this whole situation that is uncomfortable." The dance floor was not too crowded as I veered us away from the center of the floor.

"What is it that bothers you?" I asked, already sensing what the answer might be.

"Well, it sounds silly, but we are at the wedding of a woman who wanted you to father her child and sitting at a table with your first love and I don't know anyone here," she said calmly.

"Don't let it bother you," I said, as the waltz ended. "You are the most beautiful woman here and I'm glad you are with me." I was not sure what else I could say to her. I released Rebekah's hand, loosened my bow tie and unbuttoned the top button on my shirt. Rebekah stood by me with her hands folded. "We're just friends now," I said to her. "There is nothing between Annabelle and me, or Debbie and me for that matter." We started walking back towards our table.

"I know that. I'm not asking you to fix it," she said quietly. "I'm just telling you that I am uncomfortable," she concluded.

"Duly noted," I replied, trying to learn another lesson in relationships.

TWENTY-TWO

~

I sipped from the cup of coffee with my elbows leaning hard and tired on the table. I rarely drank coffee but when I did I drank French Market's chicory and I drank it motor oil black with only a little sugar. I sometimes wished I had an addiction or a love of coffee, or cigarettes, but I didn't. I wondered if it would be more defining to others, make me easier to categorize, to have an addiction of some type? It would certainly lend color to one's character. Was alcohol mine? I didn't think so. I could quit whenever I needed to do so.

I set the coffee cup down on the table. It was a little before 8:00 a.m. on Saturday morning, a week after the wedding, and I had agreed to meet Caroline for breakfast. I had chosen the Pitt Grill for a meeting place because it lacked any elitism. It was filled with people who aspired, but had not achieved, or better yet had no chance to succeed and were doing their best to hold their own against life's strong existential head wind. There were truckers, waitresses, retirees, along with the long term unemployed, the professionally unemployed, and the recently unemployed. It was a minimum wage crowd eating on well-worn hard brown plastic plates. I imagined it as a place Charles Bukowski, "Hank," would have frequented.

The parts of conversation that one would overhear suggested suspicion and conspiracy theories. The fates were always stacked against them, and, but for those conspiring against them, the politicians, the blacks, the Jews, their spouses, their bosses, they would be successful. It must have been a heavy load to carry. I recalled something that I attributed to a poem by Bukowski, that hatred is the only art of the mass man. I felt alive but alienated here. I was no longer common enough. I had unwittingly embraced, or at least danced at arm's length in my job, with middle class values. I was now part of the system. But Bukowski was right, the average man knew how to hate in abundance, though over time he had been pressured culturally into dressing it up, to try to make it and himself more palatable, as economic theory or religious requirement.

I saw Caroline walk in and raised my hand in acknowledgement as she walked toward me with a wide morning sunshine smile on her face. She slid into the booth across from me and, upon settling in, reached for my hands on the table between us and squeezed them slightly with her hands. The waitress saw her and came over and took our order. Cigarette smoke from a nearby table drifted over to us.

"You had not seen Annabelle in awhile?" Caroline asked.

"No," I replied, reaching for my ancient white coffee cup. I took another sip of the coffee and noticed a lipstick stain on the rim of the cup. The taste was now bitter in my mouth.

"I can't recall if you told me this or not, but did you date her at one time?" she asked.

"Yeah, but it's been awhile back," I replied, without emotion, as I glanced back at an elderly couple in a nearby booth. Neither had spoken to the other in the ten minutes I had seen them seated together. You could always tell the long-term married couples. They rarely spoke. The optimist would say that they knew each other so well there was no need to speak. The pessimist assumed they had nothing to talk about, living parallel lives that never intersected in any meaningful way. They were silently surviving, "praying for the end of time" as Meatloaf had sung, having long ago given up thoughts of achieving their dreams. I saw such couples in such sad terms. It was a wringing of the hands sort of existence, tied to their respective whipping posts. I thought about Annabelle as I knew her years ago.

"I know that look of yours," Caroline said empathetically. I lowered my head, as if, like a small child, I had been caught in the act of trying to steal a cookie. Caroline knew, quite often, by my expression alone whether I felt an attachment to someone. She referred to these personal attachments on my part as "spiritual." I was not offended by her characterization. In fact, I knew that I was fortunate to have had such relationships in my life.

"Was it hard for you to be around her again?" she asked me.

"Not in the sense that I think you mean," I replied slowly. "Neither of us is who we used to be. It was all a bit unreal to see her as she is now, yet to know how she was many years ago. It brought home my own compromises over the years. It was kind of like, I don't know, like she was a caricature of her former self. Maybe at some point that happens to all of us," I said, dispassionately. I wasn't pleased with my harsh sounding description, but I couldn't think of a better way to describe it. I told Caroline it had prompted me to think about how societal pressures deform us. She listened while I spoke.

The connection between Annabelle and me had been on a level that was much more intellectual than physical, a conundrum for my usual binary categories of the women who had been in my life. Allowed, perhaps, because of the beauty of her non-conformity. Quite often we had known what the other person was thinking before anything was actually said. I recalled distantly reciting from memory all of England's Kings and Queens to her with my head in her lap as she sat on the floor in her house. We had been drinking cheap wine the better part of that rainy afternoon and trying to play a game of chess. She was not a good chess player. She would often get lost in thought and forget how each piece moved.

"It's a silly game," I recall her saying. When she got too frustrated, or wanted to declare a draw, she would promptly quit, or childishly knock the chess pieces over and laugh, challenging my male need for structure.

"Well, are you going to reminisce about Annabelle or present your quotation for the day?" Caroline said with a grin. "I'll understand if it's the former." The waitress came by with our meals. I noticed as she set the plates down that the elderly couple got up to leave in silence. The older gentleman touched his wife on the arm to let her leave in front of him. She said nothing in response.

I lifted my eyes above the top of the frames of my glasses. Caroline became a blur when I did this. It had been several weeks since we had played our game of discussing a quotation. I had looked forward to doing it with her again.

"My quotation today," I started, "comes from Freud's - "

"--This is not about sex, is it?" Caroline interrupted, with a combination of playful frustration and parental disapproval etched on her face. She reached for the salt and pepper. I ignored her question and continued my sentence.

"- *The Future of an Illusion*." I paused and then opened to my bookmarker and read from the book I had brought:

> *If men are taught that there is no almighty and all-just God, no divine world order and no future life, they will feel exempt from all obligations to obey the precepts of civilization. Everyone will, without inhibition or fear, follow his asocial, egotistic instincts and seek to exercise his power. . . . Even if we knew or could prove that religion was not in possession of the truth, we ought to conceal that fact.*

I stopped reading and looked at Caroline. Caroline sat silently, mulling it over, eating her eggs as I set the book down on the table top and reached for my stained cup of coffee. I wished I had some orange juice, as the coffee taste was no longer appealing. How could people drink three and four cups a day? I looked around for the waitress, but did not see her.

"The basic question he is asking," Caroline said, slowly, as if linking the concepts in her mind one by one, "is whether there can be ethics without God." She pointed at me with her fork as she thought further. "There is nothing novel about that question," she continued, "and you are proof, at least, that one can be ethical even if the person does not believe in God." Caroline turned her attention from me to attract the waitress's attention.

"So you think it would be a safe world to live in even if the citizenry was presented proof that there was no God?" I finally asked, after we ordered some orange juice and toast from the waitress.

"It's hardly a safe world now," she stated, in a matter-of-fact tone. "I think it might be a much more despairing world without belief in God, but not more or less safe."

I always wanted to agree with that position and when Caroline said it there was an attractiveness to it, but I did not firmly hold such a conviction. For me an individual could be ethical without God, but, as Voltaire had opined, it helped if they were a philosopher, or a student of philosophy. Since most of society ignored philosophy, unless it could be condensed into cute bromidic one line quotations on daily living calendars, my faith in the masses' ability to adopt ethics on their own volition was not strong.

"But if faith in God is a reflection of lost faith in oneself, the removal of God as an alternative leaves a void in the lives of the masses. What replaces lost faith?" I asked, as I reached for the orange juice the waitress brought. Caroline sipped from a glass of water.

"I'm not sure I agree that all belief in God is a reflection of lost faith in oneself," she replied.

"Would you agree that it is in the case of the religious zealot or fanatic?" I asked, interrupting her. Again Caroline lifted the glass of water and sipped.

"I guess there are some cases where a person believes their life has become meaningless, and in their search for meaning they not only find God, but they allow religion to consume them," she replied. "That people get obsessive about something is not unique to religion," she then stated, as she leaned back in the booth. I wondered if she had ever been obsessive about anything. I ran my hand through my hair then tugged on my mustache absentmindedly.

"It doesn't cause you to question the faith of someone who admittedly finds God when their life is in total despair? Doesn't that cast doubt on the legitimacy of their decision?" I asked.

"No," Caroline replied immediately. "People come to their belief in God in innumerable ways. Sometimes it is in despair and other times it is in happiness, like the beauty of the birth of a child. The reason they come to their belief is immaterial," she said. I did not agree with Caroline. One way seemed coerced to me. I sat quietly as the waitress placed our check in front of me.

"So back to Freud's point," I said, turning to face Caroline. "How do you fill the void if there is no God for the masses?" I pulled my wallet out and thumbed through the paper money to pay the bill.

"No one can be certain," Caroline said, "but presumably people would focus on their families or their jobs ...," she said, pausing to eat a last bite of her breakfast.

"Find another cause to believe in?" I interjected, somewhat sarcastically.

"Something like that," Caroline said, without taking note of my hint of sarcasm.

"It's funny," I said. "I recall that Annabelle once asked me whether I would change the way I lived my life if they proved definitively that there was a God---and, I said no. I sometimes think that's the most intelligent question I have ever been asked about my belief system." We both began to slide out of the booth to leave.

"Well, it proves my point that whether people believe a God exists or doesn't exist, it will not alter people's attitudes such that the world will become more unsafe," Caroline replied. "I certainly would not change the basic rules by which I live my life. Of course, since there is a God this is nothing but philosophical argument," she said, with a smirk I understood.

"I'm amazed," I replied, trying to act as if I was amazed.

"That I would continue to insist there is a God?" Caroline asked, as we were walking out the restaurant.

"No, I'm amazed that you believe that people who do not believe in God are as ethical as people who do," I replied, opening the door for her to exit first.

"Believers and nonbelievers do unethical things all the time," Caroline responded. "And often they do it on behalf of what they believe in. Believers, as history unfortunately shows, don't have the market cornered on ethics."

"Amen," I replied, as we walked into the parking lot and Caroline stepped away to head to her car.

"Call me and lets you, me and Rebekah go out soon," she yelled out to me. I raised my hand to acknowledge her comment, but realized her back was already turned.

TWENTY-THREE

~

An unusual summer breeze was blowing down Oak Street. It was a Sunday afternoon at the Maple Leaf, and the Maple Leaf's weekly poetry readings, the longest running in the city, would start in an hour. The front door to the bar was open and a stale breeze whistled through it.

I felt good. My hair was in a carefully braided ponytail, the joint effort of Caroline and Rebekah. I had my favorite earring in place, the one I shared with Rebekah, my red high-top Converse tennis shoes on and comfortable worn clothes. Caroline and Rebekah were both with me seated at the bar. Rebekah had on a pair of faded blue jeans and a man's sleeveless undershirt and knee-high stiletto black leather boots. She wore no bra and it was obvious. Her reddish blonde hair fell to her waist. She had a small section of hair braided in the middle. She was sensual and slutty at the same time. It was one of the few occasions when I thought she was really comfortable in my environment.

Caroline was wearing a conservative green wrap around cotton skirt that tied at her waist and a slightly oversized white blouse. While Caroline drank Coke, Rebekah intrigued the male bartender, and doubled her mystique among the loyal male denizens, by asking him for a Pimms cup. This request sent the bartender to his Mr. Boston cocktail book to look up the recipe. Rebekah enjoyed this fact, this minor female manipulation, and winked at me as she waited. I sat between the two of them drinking a gin and tonic.

The reason for the get together was that I was contemplating reading a few of my poems. I was actually vaguely uncomfortable about it and had not decided whether I would read any. However, when I mentioned that I might, that was enough for Caroline and Rebekah to conspire to make it into an outing. Now that my summer graduate school semester had ended it was a nice break from the monotony of work.

"So are you going to read the poem about your mother?" Rebekah suddenly asked me, as she leaned on the bar waiting for the bartender to try and decipher his Mr. Boston index.

"I really don't have anything about my mother," I then replied. Rebekah referred to a poem describing a person's mother that she had read in my notebook and that she assumed it was my own mother.

I had brought that poem with me, but was surprised she recalled it. At that moment, I recited one stanza of the poem to myself:

> *I remembered it clearly now.*
> *I had told her that Pontius Pilot was*
> *the only honest man in the bible,*
> *something Nietzsche had written I think.*
> *But she did not answer and simply*
> *turned her eyes*
> *away from me,*
> *back to the black leather*
> *bible and moved*
> *her finger slowly across*
> *the page. Her lips moved as*
> *she read to herself:*
> *a silent church chant to take*
> *away the dark edges of her existence.*

"Do you see your mother often?" Caroline then asked, having heard Rebekah's reference to my mother.

"On occasion," I said, realizing that it had been several months since I had seen her, or talked with her. As if anticipating the next question, I leaned back on the barstool. "We get along fine these days. I just have no real relationship with her." Caroline sat listening. There was that familiar pained expression on her face, as if she felt something for me which I could not feel myself. I tried to bring my mother's image to mind.

It was one of the things in my life that I knew Caroline would never understand. I had no emotional attachment to my mother. At least there was no attachment that I was aware of at the time. I had often wondered why that was the case. My conclusions were incomplete, because I remembered nothing of my childhood.

Attachment theory says we attach early to a parent or caregiver. Perhaps the fact, which I was told by my father, that I was dropped off elsewhere, in the care of others, as a baby was decisive. Of the four types of attachments mine seemed to fit the Disorganized Attachment model, where there simply was no attachment, no bond which had developed.

"The only story I ever heard about my birth is that my mother was not happy about the discomforts of her first pregnancy. She was very young and she asked that they induce labor about a month early," I said. I was not sure why that story had come to me. I could sense Rebekah looking around the room as I leaned forward. Caroline's eyes, however, remained on me.

"Children ought to have a great caring story about their birth," Caroline said sympathetically to me, as Rebekah excused herself to go to the restroom. Tinsley Ellis' *Quitters Never Win* began to play on the juke box.

"That's a good observation," I replied, thinking of the quote I attributed to Shakespeare to be careful of the stories you tell yourself as you may end up living them. It probably applies equally to the stories told to a child by their parents.

The wounds of my childhood, the acts or omissions of my parents, such as they were, seemed distant to me. They were my responsibility now, my burden, I told myself. My story to unpack, rewrite or reinvent. Still I had a growing unease that I needed to learn more about it, about these stories I had been told. I thought the feeling stemmed solely from my desire to know myself and the reasons for some of my actions. I had only a vague sense of the connectivity of one's childhood environment and one's abilities, or lack thereof, to function within an intimate relationship later in life.

The poetry readings lasted for about two hours. Encouraged by Caroline and Rebekah, I read two poems, including the one referring to my mother. It was an odd experience exposing oneself for the approval of others. I had no trouble discussing issues in an intellectual fashion, but my poetry was personal. It was my unfiltered and unformed emotions and I had not developed the armor to accompany the reactions to it. To reveal it was to reveal myself in a vulnerable state. The reception seemed positive, but I puzzled over why I did it. It seemed an unnecessary risk.

TWENTY-FOUR

~

I woke up early the following Sunday morning with a heaviness in my eyes, groggy with the rising sun, as if I had slept too much. Rebekah was again out of town for work, but was returning that evening. I felt overwhelmingly tired as I moved stiff and shuffled barefoot around the kitchen in the early morning.

I got undressed, mechanically, and then showered. While standing in the shower, letting the water run over me, I was suddenly struck by the idea that I should go to church. I finished showering and found myself going through the motions of getting dressed to do so. I checked the paper for the mass times at a nearby Catholic church. What was prompting me? What bargain with my despair was I seeking? I guess I was motivated, subconsciously, by the grace and peace religious belief seemed to provide Caroline. I needed some of that peace.

I drove to the church and sat in an empty pew in the back. I waited as the sparsely attended service began. I waited through the initial greetings from the priest, through the altar boys ringing bells, through the historical symbolic rituals that I recalled remotely from my adolescence, through the readings from the gospels. Nothing happened. There was no moment of inspiration. No moment of grace. There was no moment of transcendence. No uplift in my emotion. It was no different than if I had chosen, instead, to go to the grocery store that

morning. I left the church silently, unchanged, as the commu-
nion services began.

TWENTY-FIVE

~

I sat on the porch steps at my house early the next morning prior to leaving for work and looked out at the yellow oak pollen which was blanketing my car and everything else in sight. The seed pods would eventually rain down just as actively, signaling the end of this elaborate dance of nature which I did not understand, but which I observed annually through watery eyes and with a runny nose.

Rebekah was still asleep. There was a slightly cool breeze which was blowing intermittently before a complete sunrise. I sat outside without a shirt in my boxer shorts. A summer morning chill came over me. It was unexpected. It reminded me of the early morning chill on my face upon waking in poorly insulated college rent houses during the winter. I reflected on the past few weeks. I wrapped my arms tightly about my torso hoping to generate some body heat.

In seeing Annabelle again, it dawned on me how unnecessarily complicated my life had become. I missed the real or perceived simplicity of our past life together, of our shared intellectual heresy. Was the past actually as I thought, or was it just an imagined glorious one created by my current needs? Since I had begun practicing law the rituals of socializing had become increasingly regimented and stressful to me. I chafed at the bit, at the conformity it required of me. Perhaps it was because certain people who entered my life were now categorized as "business clients," or potential clients. This was a

categorization of people that had not previously existed in my
life; a persona, in response, that I had never had to create. I
tried to treat clients like friends, taking them to dinner, ball
games, and other events. However, unlike socializing with a
true friend, you were supposed to be monitoring the client's
reaction to see that he or she was enjoying themselves. I
resisted.

Maybe some of those clients would become friends, but
I couldn't see that yet. I was never very good at pretending,
apparently had not developed the right filters, and it struck me
as an unnecessary expenditure of my energy. Right or wrong,
I decided I would just be me from now on and hope that my
legal competence would clear any social or business obstacle.
If you were good at your job, I thought, your differences would
just be considered idiosyncrasies. If you were not good at your
job those differences would be further proof that you were not
good at your job.

As I thought about it, it seemed to me that it had been a
long time since I had gotten together with a group of friends
without ambition and simply forgotten all the socially imposed
rules. My dealings with Caroline had become the only exceptions. Some of those early friendships, that we were sure would
last forever, had rusted and fallen away into disrepair. Too often
I was the one keeping in contact, maintaining the friendship,
reaching out, and then suddenly it seemed I tired of the effort and started to excommunicate people for real or perceived
infractions.

I recognized at the time I had decided to go to law school
that if I was not careful I might become exactly what I had
always rebelled against, but felt confident in my ability to with-
stand the pressures and stand apart. Once I started practicing
law I felt the societal sandpaper grind against the rough edges
of my non-conformity. I had gotten my ear pierced at the time

I entered law school so I would never forget. Nevertheless there were times when I felt that my vigilance had failed.

Had I become Jackson Browne's Pretender, the "happy idiot struggling for the legal tender?" I wasn't comfortable with the thought. It seemed to me the only thing I could do was to try to stay conscious of it and limit, or resist, the compromises. That was an important concept for me anyway, to try and stay conscious of the absurd. A cool breeze blew up again and I decided to go inside and get dressed for work.

TWENTY-SIX

~

The following week a tropical storm developed overnight in the Gulf of Mexico. I listened to the rustling of the large brown Magnolia leaves on the sidewalk from a gentle breeze. I'm sure my elderly neighbors would have preferred that I raked up the leaves in my front yard, making it more presentable, but I purposely chose not to do so. It wasn't mean spirited, it was simply that I liked the sound, the movement of the leaves in dance with the wind. The breeze would be picking up as the night wore on, as the tropical storm was supposed to make landfall about 80 miles away in Biloxi, Mississippi. It was not a very strong storm, with the quixotic name of Imelda, but New Orleans would probably get 40-50 mile per hour wind gusts from the outer bands of the storm. In all likelihood, we would lose the electricity for a few hours during the night. I welcomed the imposed darkness.

The sound of the leaves in motion on the sidewalk was the first sign of the approaching storm. I sat at the kitchen table and listened in the dark. I could feel the darkness in an audible way. It engulfed me, hid me, and supported me like some shadowed hand that I had sought out. The electricity was not out yet, but it was after midnight and I had turned off all the lights, preferring to sit in the dark. Caroline was sleeping over, and I had chosen to sit up while she slept. I had the kitchen windows open and the breeze was cool, damp and varying. It had a scent that was full of its potential fury.

Rebekah and I had reached an agreement about tropical storms and hurricanes. She would leave town and I stayed behind. Since she was not a native New Orleanian, she had not yet been anesthetized by the process over the many years. Indeed, she was as unnerved by hurricanes as by my desire to stay behind. She was frightened and I was not very comforting. It was one of the compromises that relationships foist upon us, the trail of small white lies and minor deceptions that too often alter who we are. Until one day we awaken, if we awake at all, as if from a long-induced sleep, look around, and wonder how we became who we are. But as was often the case I more or less staked out my position, in this case that I was not leaving, and she then made her decision. I forced her hand because, in my own insecurity, I did not really understand the nature of a relationship and still saw it, too often, as something where you won or you lost and there was a silent scorekeeper.

When I thought of Rebekah, as I sat in the dark, my stomach knotted. It was a feeling I could not explain.

The rain started to come down lightly outside. I thought about lighting a candle and decided not to do so, preferring the darkness. The storm whimpered its way along the coast and into Mississippi. I didn't lose electricity.

TWENTY-SEVEN

~

Caroline had told me that she was going to bring me a copy of Loretta's dissertation in Clinical Psychology to read. She thought that I might enjoy reading it considering the nature of the topic. I had not thought about it since the time that Caroline, staying over during the storm, had first mentioned it. After asking again if I was interested in reading it, and obtaining my assent, she had given it to me in a large, worn, manila envelope one night at the Maple Leaf. I do not know if Loretta was aware that Caroline had given me a copy to read. I brought it home and put it on the kitchen table that night without opening the envelope.

Several days later, and after being asked by Caroline if I had read it yet, I finally came home and pulled it out of the envelope. It's not that I wasn't interested in reading it. My reading habits ran in spurts. I loved to read, truly loved to read, in a way that was hard to explain to others. Books were part of my identity, a necessary affirmation that, perhaps, started as a child. The books which littered my house sustained me. At certain times I would read 3-4 books a month. Then the intense desire to sit alone and read would leave me for weeks or months at a time. Of late I had simply not been in the mood.

I looked down at the envelope with the dissertation in it. I guess my attitude toward psychology was consistent with growing up with an ex-Marine as a father in a Sicilian-Catholic family. Although I was, perhaps, a little more progressive than my ancestors, I still thought, at that time, that most of what psychology labeled as mental illness was nothing more than problems of existence. Psychology, like so many other things, had expanded its base with the general public by exonerating everyone of responsibility for their actions. Hence, the endless expansion by the profession of what constituted "mental illness." It was maddening to me that we existed in a culture that constantly created new excuses for avoiding being responsible for one's own actions. In that regard, it reminded me of organized religion pandering to the lowest common denominator, to the least capable, and offering a better life in the hereafter if only you joined the club and paid some attention to the rules.

Loretta's dissertation was entitled "The Effects of Generational Secrets." Something about the title struck a positive, but remote, response within me. Being from an immigrant family I had a strong, though unfocused, sense of generational importance. Ancestors from the "old country" were often mythical figures, like my father's father, who journeyed heroically long distances at young ages. Standing next to the kitchen table, I lifted up the paper and thumbed a few pages into the paper and read on the second page of the introduction:

> *Secrets are often passed down from one generation of a family to the next. Whole families unknowingly tilt in directions designed to preserve the secret and protect the perpetrator. Their collective character and sometimes the content of their individual character changes form to preserve the secret.*

> *Sometimes the secrets which are maintained are simple like a pregnancy that resulted out of wedlock. Other times the secret is more insidious like sexual molestation or abuse by a grandparent or parent. Whatever its form, the*

secret gains life in the dark and quickly burrows beneath the surface of familial relationships like the head of a tick in search of food. After the secret is safely secured beneath the surface, it begins to control and define the relationships of the perpetrator, of those protecting the perpetrator and even those unaware of the secret's existence. What started as embarrassment, or a concern over appearance, congeals into a conspiracy to conceal. The individuals are bonded by the secret, even when unaware of its existence.

Those unaware of the secret may become unwitting accomplices by cutting off access to the secret in a misguided attempt to protect the keeper of the secret from pain. This is an inculcated and learned behavior. The keeper of the secret, or the entire family, may, like one of Tolkien's characters, transform over time, because of the secret and the energy spent preserving it, from a lovable Hobbit to an excrescent Gollum.

I set the paper back down on the table, pulled the chair back from the table and then sat down. The introduction sounded like a familial version of Jung's collective unconscious, instincts and structures of thought that are shared by mankind. A distant memory stirred again within me. I sat listening, but could not bring the memory forward, like a word I almost remembered but was then lost to the quick death of my cells. I felt a bit uneasy, but could not tell why. I sensed that my heartbeat had quickened. I scratched my right forearm reflexively, as I often did as a nervous habit. I adjusted the chair toward the table and began reading the paper at the beginning.

TWENTY-EIGHT

~

D on't forget the partnership meeting at 1:30," Melinda said to me, in a cautionary tone, as I left my office for lunch.

"I won't," I replied, walking slowly past her desk. I could smell her perfume. I knew so little about such feminine things like perfumes. I am sure she wore a popular brand, but I realized I could not name even one brand of men's cologne or women's perfume. I smiled at her slightly to convey that I both understood her need to remind me and my appreciation of her organizational skills.

I headed out of the office down the street to the Commerce Restaurant, a nearby sandwich shop. The sandwich shop was one of the very few left in town where I could get a scrambled egg po-boy without the need to explain the order. I ordered the po-boy and sat down at a table to wait for my name to be called out indicating the order was ready.

The Commerce Restaurant only had six tables and a counter with three stools. Each table had a disposable aluminum ashtray on it. The restaurant was heavy with cigarette smoke. A small black and white TV was sitting on the bar top tuned to the local midday news. The TV picture was turned to face the lady sitting in a chair behind the cash register.

Ms. Clara had been seated behind that cash register for a life time. She knew my order by heart and often had it rung up before I had the chance to tell her what I had ordered. She would spin on her chair and grab me a long-neck Barq's out of the metal cooler and then tell me what my bill was.

After eating and walking around for a few minutes, I returned to the office. As I walked past Melinda she silently pointed to the conference room where the partnership meeting was being held. I immediately understood her pointing to mean that the partners were already in the room. Instead of heading to my office, I walked directly to the conference room.

The meeting had not yet begun. Davalier and Johnson, senior partners, were seated at the far end of the conference room table. I glanced around and it appeared to me that all 11 partners were present.

An agenda was passed around while Johnson blathered on about his recent encounter with a local judge at a CLE in the Bahamas. After a few minutes Johnson concluded his story and began to discuss the first item on the agenda.

The issues on the agenda at partnership meetings were normally of little interest to me. I scanned the agenda for today's meeting and it was similarly uninspiring.

The first issue to be discussed was the firm's vacation policy for staff. Johnson stated that the senior partners were proposing that staff be given one week per year up to a total of three weeks. Johnson then stated that the senior partners were also in agreement that though this was going to be the stated policy any senior partner could give additional days off, above the three weeks, to staff faced with a need for more time. Johnson then asked that the matter be voted on.

A junior partner's role at such a meeting was to keep quiet and to take his lead from the position the senior partners proposed. For my part, I generally complied with this role, mostly because I had no interest in the issues discussed. However, on this occasion I knew immediately why Johnson was pushing a corollary to the stated vacation policy. It was rumored that

Johnson was having an affair with his secretary. The ability of a senior partner to unilaterally give additional days off was simply a vehicle to allow for rewarding secretaries involved with a senior partner.

At Johnson's suggestion, the proposal was put to a vote. I did not vote when he called for those in favor to say "aye." The other partners all voted in favor. Johnson was looking at me during the vote and I knew that he was aware that I did not vote. He did not call for anyone voting in the negative.

The next issue on the agenda concerned minimum hourly billings per month for associates. We were all aware that Johnson and Davalier had been pushing for a minimum number of billing hours per month which associates would be required to meet. However, Singleton and Slayton, the two other senior partners, had been opposed to the proposal. I was not in favor of setting minimums because I believed it encouraged people to pad their billable hours.

A discussion between the senior partners ensued on the issue. It was mostly a friendly discussion with no participation by the junior partners. At the end of the discussion, and to my surprise, Johnson asked for me to express my opinion on the issue. It was clear to me that he thought by putting me on the spot I might be too intimidated to oppose him.

"I think a minimum will lead people to further exaggerate their billable hours," I said bluntly, unconcerned with the ramification of my remark. Not only had I been interjected into a dispute between senior partners, but I had now mentioned an issue, that of padding of billing hours, which was purposely ignored by most of the partners. The air conditioner could be heard, in the sudden silence, rushing air through the vents overhead.

"Are you aware of any lawyers currently padding their hours?" Johnson asked, sweeping his hand across the table, while making hurried and anxious eye contact with several of the other partners. I knew from his expression that Johnson, who had a habit of being confrontational, was trying to provoke me.

"There are partners and associates who exaggerate their actual hours," I said, matter-of-factly. "You know it and I know it." Mr. Slayton, who generally did not take himself, or such meetings, too seriously, chuckled at my remark. Johnson put both of his hands on the conference table and then clenched them into fists. He looked disapprovingly at Slayton. Davalier leaned back in his chair and folded his arms as he looked at me. I realized, perhaps too late, that I was again placing my career at the firm in jeopardy.

"Suppose you tell all of us about these facts that you believe you have uncovered. Tell us who these partners and associates are who you claim are padding their hours. Enlighten us?" Johnson said, in an increasingly agitated tone.

I looked directly at him before I spoke. My face, I was sure, showed no emotion. The curtain had fallen.

"Everyone in this room knows whom I am speaking about," I said. "I simply have the balls to raise the subject." Slayton smiled into his hands.

"You got fuckin' balls!" Johnson sneered as he stood up. "Well enlighten us, tell us all about these criminals," Johnson then insisted, as his chair fell backwards to the floor. Again I did not immediately respond. Davalier reached awkwardly from his chair to try and pick up Johnson's fallen chair. Johnson was losing his temper, something he did often whenever challenged.

"I'll give you one example," I finally said, as calmly as I could. I purposely waited, kept him uncomfortable, while he remained standing. "I had occasion to see last month's bills which my secretary Melinda typed for Mr. Davalier," I said.

Davalier now leaned forward in his chair and looked at me as if he had just learned, prior to his criminal trial's commencement, that his co-conspirator, me, had been given immunity in exchange for his damaging testimony. "On three separate days last month Davalier billed 24 hours per day," I said. Slayton again laughed quietly to himself. The other partners remained quiet.

"This is absurd," Davalier said, red-faced.

"I agree. I agree!" Johnson promptly replied, sitting down in the chair Davalier had set back up.

"You don't know what you saw on any of those bills," Davalier responded, ridiculously, pointing his finger at me.

"Maybe I need new glasses," I said sarcastically. "Why don't we pull the bills right now so we can all see if I'm right?" I asked rhetorically, knowing full well that would not happen. Johnson looked like he was going to become unhinged at my remarks. Before either Davalier, Johnson or I spoke again, Mr. Slayton interrupted.

"We're not going to resolve any of this right now. Let's just vote on this issue and move on," he said. There was an angry moment of quiet before Johnson called for a vote on the issue. The vote was 8 - 3 with Singleton, Slayton and myself voting against the measure.

Several more items on the agenda were discussed. On two or three occasions Johnson and Davalier looked at me as if they were going to say something to me. I did not speak again at the meeting. At 3:30 the meeting ended and I exited the office quickly without speaking to anyone and looking forward to the weekend. I knew as I left, however, that I had set in motion Johnson and Davalier attempting to have me fired.

TWENTY-NINE

~

I guess I never tended to think of Caroline in sexual terms. I knew, however, that she would be offended if I had ever said that to her directly. I did not believe that she had any amorous intentions toward me, or about converting our relationship to something more than a friendship. Nevertheless, I had never discussed with her the subject of my perceptions of her sexuality. Even if a woman is just your friend, I decided years ago, it's never a good idea to tell them you view them as a nonsexual entity. I recalled being told by a female friend, I occasionally slept with when I was young, that "sex was irrelevant to our friendship." Although true, that stung, and I'm sure being told she was not sexy by me would have felt the same.

There was, however, no sexual attraction between us from my perspective. I realized that she dated on occasion. Mostly it seemed to me that she would go out with someone on two or three occasions and then the "dating," such as it was, would end. However, I could not recall ever meeting anyone whom she dated. On one or two occasions, when we were out on the weekends, she had pointed someone out to me as a former date.

Caroline, I also knew, was a virgin. She was a virgin because she felt her religious beliefs required it until she married. On occasion when I chided her about this she would point out in emphatic tones that this did not mean she was "non-orgasmic." I was never exactly certain what she was trying to convey to me, and, in my rare embarrassment, decided not to question her directly about it. I would simply nod in the affirmative when she offered such a qualification. I always assumed that her dating relationships ended when the guy realized she wasn't kidding about her commitment to being a virgin.

In any event, I listened to Caroline and Rebekah talking in the living room and could hear that they were talking about dating and about men. I was laying on the bed and had just awakened from a Saturday afternoon nap. I assumed that Caroline had stopped by while I was asleep. I heard the ice fall against the side of a glass as someone set it down on the coffee table in the living room.

Rebekah had always treated Caroline with respect. The friendship that had slowly developed between them appeared to me to be genuine. I was glad that the two of them got along so well. It was difficult to tell, however, how the relationship between them was defining itself. On occasion Rebekah acted as a big sister might act toward Caroline. On other occasions Caroline would talk to Rebekah about some issue in almost motherly tones. Each of them played a variety of roles with the other. I thought that was unusual. Stereotypically it seemed to me that most women didn't trust other women, though they would pretend otherwise. Perhaps the female distrust was an evolutionary competitive leftover.

Rebekah, I knew from our conversations, admired the strength of Caroline's religious and personal convictions. She saw a discipline in Caroline's character that she often commented was missing in most human beings.

Caroline, on the other hand, admired the same characteristics in Rebekah. While Rebekah applauded Caroline's conviction toward her religious beliefs, including her virginity, Caroline was genuinely impressed with the fact that Rebekah made choices in her life, including living with someone, despite any familial or religious pressure not to do so. There was silence in the living room.

I heard Caroline tell Rebekah about her father, who was a Colonel in the Army, and that her mother was usually deferential to his authority. I then heard Rebekah's voice.

"A man needs to be treated at all times by the woman in his life as if he is unique and not like any other man she has ever known, especially in the way he treats her. All men need that approval." I heard a soft laugh from Rebekah and then several more words from her which I could not understand. I could imagine Caroline sitting next to Rebekah with a smile on her face. I lay quietly and listened. The sheets against my side as I turned were cool and dry. I did not hear a reply from Caroline and I gradually fell back asleep.

THIRTY

$\sim$

I was running late for meeting Caroline after work. She had asked that I meet her at a coffee shop on Julia Street about three blocks from where my office was located. I had to finish revising a legal brief to be filed the next morning in the local state Court of Appeals and it had taken longer than I thought it would. I wasn't satisfied with the second draft of the brief, so I rewrote and reorganized an entire section of it. I always wrote as if I had to read what I wrote out loud. It was the closest thing I had to a writing "style." If it sounded good to my ear being read out loud it was generally well written. The reading out loud approach was undoubtedly the product of missing too many grammar classes in high school. I had never learned to diagram sentences, didn't really know what a pronoun was or an adverb. I had, however, read a lot even as a kid and that undoubtedly taught me how to write.

Unlike the other lawyers in our office, I also always wrote things out long hand. I never used a Dictaphone. It was somehow rooted in my general aversion to technology. I thought that such technology simply separated us from the necessary immersion in our mental processes.

It was 1991 and I had still never been to a coffee shop before. The idea of a shop specializing in coffee reminded me of scenes from Paris described in the series of novels I had read by Sartre. I would have never guessed that the concept was transferable to America, except to the extent that it became fashionable. If a concept becomes fashionable, there is always some segment of society willing to embrace it in a search for temporary transcendence, and make it part of their "culture."

I walked into the shop, which was brightly lit, and saw Caroline seated at a small corner table dressed in a halter type top and a flowered skirt. She smiled as I approached and stood up to kiss me before I sat down. The smell of freshly ground coffee beans was pungent in the air.

"How was your day?" she asked.

"Nothing exciting," I said, looking around the coffee shop as I sat down. "I had to rewrite a brief. Sorry if I am late," I said.

She looked at her watch for a moment as if she had not realized I was late. Unlike me who lived my life, and was confined, by the practice of law, in billable six minute increments, Caroline never seemed aware of time. It had not captured or restricted her as it did so many of us at various stages of our lives.

She asked me what I was going to do that night. I told her that I had no plans, but that I needed to eat soon.

We left the coffee shop as the waitress was coming to take my order. We drove together to a small restaurant named "Mona Lisa's" on Royal Street near the outskirts of the French Quarter. The restaurant did not yet have its liquor license so I went across the street, bought an inexpensive bottle of Cabernet and returned with it to the restaurant. I handed the waitress the bottle of wine in a brown paper bag. She took the wine into the kitchen area of the restaurant, uncorked the bottle, decanted it, and returned it to our table with two glasses.

I poured the wine slowly until both of our glasses were half filled. Before long, and through much conversation, we had emptied the contents of the bottle. I went across the street to retrieve another bottle. It was a humid night and the scent of the Mississippi river was in the air. Caroline was in good spirits and seemed to laugh at everything I said. It was reassuring. After a while, however, she began to quiz me about the details of my relationship with Rebekah.

"Do you think you will ever get married?" she asked.

"Rebekah wants to, but I can't see it happening," I replied.

"Do you love her?" Caroline asked, as she gently tapped a finger on the table.

"I do," I said too quickly. I hesitated. "At least I think I do." I ran my hand through the hair on the right side of my head. It was still a troubling issue for me and I had not recalled discussing it with Caroline.

"If you love her, why don't you marry her?" Caroline then asked. I laughed slightly and wished for a moment that such simple syllogisms were always correct.

"That sounds like a religious question," I replied.

"It wasn't meant to be," she said seriously, lifting her glass of wine to her lips.

Oddly, I thought of a quotation my father used to say with regularity about my mother: "You can love somebody and not be able to live with them." Perhaps that was his syllogism. I realized I was living with Rebekah, but that I had not thought about living with her forever. "Forever" was a meaningless concept to me, one of too many ritualized platitudes we were taught to embrace.

"Besides, I don't see any reason to get married unless you want to have kids, and I don't," I said. I didn't want to tell Caroline about my reservations over my relationship with Rebekah. It really was a matter between Rebekah and myself and I knew it was the kind of thing that would hurt Rebekah if she ever knew I had talked to Caroline about it. Nevertheless, I was tempted to get it off my chest and talk to someone about it.

Caroline started talking about old age and dying. It took me a few moments to adjust to the new topic.

Caroline had a depth of compassion toward others which was always amazing to me. As I thought about that compassion, she started to make some sort of proposal about free education programs for the elderly. My mind began to drift, and again, I thought of Rebekah. The waitress brought out our meal and we ate in relative quiet. The alcohol was taking effect on me.

"I hope I die before I get old," I sang in a low voice to myself. It struck me as soon as the words were out of my mouth that The Who considered thirty old when they had written the song. I noticed that Caroline had stopped eating and was just staring at me. She became more serious in her mannerisms and expression.

"Why would you want to die?" she asked. "Since you don't believe in God, you should want to live forever."

"I don't believe in the good old Catholic heaven, but that doesn't dictate how long I want to live," I said. I could feel the effect of the alcohol again. I felt like I wanted to talk. "If I have any right, it ought to be to decide when to die," I said.

"Now you are talking about the right to commit suicide," Caroline said, to indicate to me that my thought process was wandering off track. She was right, but it didn't stop me from rambling. I spoke for a little while longer and then finished off the last of the wine. I wasn't hungry anymore. Caroline, on the other hand, ate like it was going to be her last meal. She was so small. I don't know where she put the food.

After the meal, I dropped Caroline off and went home. It was a little after 9:00 p.m. when I walked into the house. I could hear the shower running which told me Rebekah had returned to town. I always had trouble keeping track of her travels and forgotten she would be home. I got undressed in the bedroom and joined her in the shower.

It turned out to be a typical night sexually with Rebekah. After sex in the shower, we dried off and moved onto the sofa and, ultimately, the living room floor. We both fell asleep on the floor.

After an hour or so I woke up. I moved Rebekah's head off my shoulder, got up and walked over to the black and white television and turned it on. The screen remained blank for a while as the tubes warmed up. Eventually both sound and picture came on. Surprisingly, the Three Stooges were on. Rebekah woke up about halfway through the episode I was watching. She walked into the other room for a moment and then returned.

"We need to talk," she said, standing in the doorway to the living room. Her strawberry blonde hair fell over her right shoulder and partially covered one of her breasts. I got up and turned the television off.

"You just don't ever seem happy with me. The relationship seems to be a burden to you. I feel like I am in the way," she continued, as I looked at her while standing by the television. I awkwardly moved back to the sofa feeling vulnerable. "If you want me to move out, just tell me," she said. Her ability to sense what had been on the fringe of my thinking, but still unclear, surprised me. I thought I had masked these incomplete feelings.

I stumbled a bit for words. Although I had intermittently thought about this speech, I felt unprepared. I also briefly thought about our recent lovemaking and recalled that many of my relationships had ended after particularly exhausting lovemaking.

"I just don't think it's working out like I had hoped," I finally said, flat, unemotional. As soon as I said it, the words seemed wrong and intentionally hurtful. There was an awkward and silent moment.

Rebekah began to cry. I felt terrible and a bit confused over my actions. I realized that I could not bring forth any tears.

Why was I ending a relationship with someone I felt I was in love with? I held her for a while as she cried. She leaned into me and then abruptly pulled away and wept into both of her hands. We talked some more and she calmed down.

"I don't know what it is....I love you, but my stomach hurts. I...sometimes feel trapped. Damn childhood stuff," I said, in clipped phrases, trying to explain my feelings to both of us. I could sense that the emotional part of me was trying to break out of its cage. I clamped down on it with all the intellectual discipline I could muster.

"I'm not smart enough," she said, sniffling, and with an air of resignation.

"It's not intelligence Rebekah, it's, maybe, spheres of interest. I mean, I love poetry, you don't. I enjoy reading about history and philosophy. You don't." I realized that I sounded too cold, too analytical.

"It sounds to me like you're saying I'm not smart enough. Just dressing it up like you do," she said, as she bit lightly into her trembling lower lip. She shed a few more tears. I shook my head 'no.'

"And don't forget your troubles with relationships. Maybe you just haven't tried hard enough," she countered. Part of me felt she might be right. Maybe it wasn't a question of effort, but instead lack of ability, a lack of empathy, or maybe a fear of exposing myself. But the suffocating feeling, the emerging need for distance, which I knew from my experience in other relationships, was real.

We both fell quiet for a few moments as we faced each other holding hands. She started to cry again and pulled her hands from mine as she got off the sofa. She disappeared into the other room. I did not follow her. I wanted to be elsewhere. She emerged a few moments later dressed. She moved hurried-ly, expectant, through the room. She grabbed her keys off the coffee table and stood before me fumbling for the right key on the key ring. She was no longer crying. She had regained her composure, the adult in the room.

"I'm going to spend the night at my sister's. I'll pick up my things in the next few days when you are at work." She paused. I felt I should say something, but could not find any words. "I know this is not easy for you," she said. "Somewhere in that head of yours, that processes out all of your emotions, you are struggling." She looked down at her keys. "I hope you find peace one day. There is more good in you than you realize. And maybe if you could ever recognize that, it would be a start," she then said, already forgiving me. She turned and without waiting for a reply, walked out the front door. I got off the sofa, heard her car start and stood in the middle of the living room listening to the car backing out of the driveway.

I noted that as she left the musty smell of the carpet was in the air. I heard the jolt of the shocks on Rebekah's car as she backed over the curb at the end of the driveway. I searched for feeling, but felt nothing. I was appropriately naked.

THIRTY-ONE

~

There would be no storybook ending. The house was gradually emptied of her belongings. There was no background music to the ending of the relationship, like in the movies. It simply ended. The ghost of our once shared dreams would appear periodically in the future, as a memory, and over time its well intentioned moorings would loosen and drift away.

At times over the next few days and weeks I had an odd physical sensation of which my mind was acutely aware. It felt like the symptoms of a pending heart attack. There was a tremendous weight which I periodically felt pressing down on my chest, as if I was lying down and someone was seated on top of me. There was also a vacuum, or an emptiness, which, at other moments, I felt. My stomach was in an uncomfortable knot and I was borderline nauseated. The vacuum, the sense of loss, was metaphysical, but also very palpable, created by Rebekah's absence. My poor emotional state, which I tried to keep at arm's length, was actually having a physical effect upon me. I understood this, in a vague way, from other relationships I had ended over the years. Like being seasick I knew these feelings would remain with me until I got into calm waters. Still, that knowledge, in and of itself, was not comforting to me.

My breathing was sometimes difficult and in unsteady gulps. When this happened, I felt like I could not inhale to the complete capacity of my lungs. It was odd, but I was very conscious of the mechanics of my breathing. I felt it in my ears. It was a cotton echo, as if my fingers had been placed into each ear while I inhaled and exhaled. I thought of those yoga breathing exercises Rebekah had taken as a form of meditation that she had offered to show me and which I had declined.

It is amazing how a relationship creates its own culture. I was aware of this in a piecemeal fashion from every brief relationship. There are rituals between the parties and there is symbolism in the actions of the parties which develop throughout the course of the relationship. There is an unacknowledged structure, most often framed by the issues which each of the parties brings to the relationship. There is freedom and there is restriction within that structure. There is personal definition provided by the structure. It is a definition that is in addition to what each person individually has at the inception of the relationship. Sometimes the definition is supportive and other times pernicious, overwhelming and replacing the individual. There is also the unique language of the relationship which is both verbal and physical.

I sat on the sofa and felt the cool air from the circulating ceiling fan on my arms. There would be no more morning showers together. There would be no more lovemaking on the kitchen table. There would be no more of her breath on my back in the morning. There would be no more laying in bed, quizzing each other about the significance of a dream, or her disapproval of me getting up too early on weekends.

The language created between us, the language of two lovers, would now be lost. Certain words, which had special meaning between us, would no longer have that meaning. We would use pieces of that language in future relationships, guarding or forgetting its genesis, perhaps accidentally provoking jealousy in a future lover, but it would never be quite the same. It would never be understood in the same fashion. There would be no further implementation of the customs of the relationship: decompressing conversations when returning from work, a hug before leaving in the morning, legs draped across each other while sleeping, making coffee for her while she slept so she would have some when she awoke and I was gone.

The artifacts of the relationship's unique cultural world would, by and large, be removed, destroyed or forgotten. There was her hair in the carpet and on the sofa which would be vacuumed away over the following weeks. There was her scent on the pillows and sheets to be washed away. There was her taste in my mouth on occasion which was her kiss. I sat silent as these thoughts powered into me. Yet I still did not understand. I could not yet understand. Despite it all, in my mind, I had escaped, whatever that meant. So I fell back on the comforting rituals of my own narrative.

I took my braided ponytail out from under my shirt collar and slowly unbraided it. My hair was still damp from an earlier shower. The strands then hung in ringlets to the area between the bottom of my shoulder blades. I got up from the sofa and, as if led by instinct, I searched through the bathroom cabinet and found the small silver loop earring. I looked into the bathroom mirror and put the earring through the hole in my ear. I noticed that there was light stubble on my face from a day without shaving. I returned to the living room and quickly located the album I was thinking about. The one left as a present at my house in law school by a blonde who I spent one night with before she moved back to New York. I listened to a few songs from Joni Mitchell's "For The Roses." As Joni Mitchell sang about the "blonde in the bleachers," I left the house in search of a safe place on a barstool at the Maple Leaf.

THIRTY-TWO

∾

After a week or so, my uncertainty over ending the relationship would leave me for days at a time. I found that I enjoyed the freedom of not being in the relationship. At least that's how I understood it. I had a smothering weight lifted off me. It was not necessarily the weight of the relationship but was, more precisely, the heaviness of trying to force my constantly resistant form into a certain shape, an alien shape that constituted "Us," a shape that society dictated as necessary in order to be whole. Perhaps it was the relief of not having to confront my own demons, a way to avoid whatever those entangled relationship issues were. Dealing with the devil you know is infinitely more comforting than confronting the unknown, the devil I still did not know. I never troubled over spending the time necessary to try and process my actions, but where relationships were concerned I had no ideas as to why I did what I did, what I was protecting. It was almost like sleepwalking. Someone told you that you did it, you didn't recall it and, as a result, could not begin to understand it. Still I knew something malignant lurked beneath the skin of my new contentment.

My mood would parallel the existence or nonexistence of the weight that I felt and the struggle to understand it. When it was there, I kept to myself. During those times I was not only silent, but my brain seemed to work less, like a breaker in the circuitry of my brain had switched off to avoid being overloaded. I would listen to tapes of Carlos Nakai playing the native American flute. I drank alone at the end of the bar. When the weight was gone, I would take a walk, or meet Caroline out for dinner and talk sparingly. But I could still function.

The mixture of emotions seemed odd, although not unfamiliar, to me. I was sad and happy at the same time. It was like those New Orleans afternoons when the sun was out and it was raining. The closest I would come to losing control of my emotions was when I ended a relationship. But this time it seemed different. This time it all seemed harder to control. My emotions strained hard to free themselves from my analytical cage without success, but, in the process, produced physical manifestations.

Within a few weeks, I was actually noticing and speaking to other women, seeking affirmation and relevance again.

THIRTY-THREE

~

It was raining hard outside. The rain was coming down in big drops. The rainwater ran quickly and noisily down the street near the curb into the culvert outside my house. I could smell the rain on the pavement. It reminded me briefly of the smell of the water and fish being cleaned on the back of a boat on an early morning boat launch at Blackie Campo's at Shell Beach. I had the back door of the house open, but the screen door closed, so that the breeze from the rainstorm would circulate into the house.

Still, it was hot and humid inside. I took my shirt off and, wearing only shorts, sat at the kitchen table close to the screen door. I put some ice in a glass and filled it with some $2.99 red wine left behind by a recent visitor. I could not recall who had left the wine behind. I looked at the bottle, but did not recognize the brand. I thought of Gautier who had a talent, when neither of us had money, of being able to pick out good cheap wine. He had also taught me how to uncork a bottle of wine without a corkscrew. I recalled him striking the bottom of a wine bottle on a tree trunk thereby creating pressure within the bottle and slowly forcing the cork out. I wondered where he was hitchhiking to these days and hoped he was safe.

Work was suffocating me and I knew it. The tension in the office between me, Johnson and Davalier was obvious to everyone. I had rarely spoken to either of them, except when necessary, since the blow up at the partnership meeting. They had treated me cordially, but coolly, since that time. It was tough, however, to separate the stress of work from the occasional grief over the end of the relationship with Rebekah. I was not sure if I had buried my grief, or had dealt with it. And there was something else trying to force its way out, to confront and undermine me, though I did not know what it was. I was increasingly aware of it not as an emotional response, but rather as a lack of one, a numbing void in me, the ongoing battle of my intellect and emotion, with my intellect as the temporary victor, but my nascent emotions exacting an increasingly high price for the victory.

I heard the rain intensify and looked over at the screen door. The rain was being driven into the screen. The water began to bead up on the screen. I watched, disinterested, without getting up.

It was bothersome to me that people who I perceived as more limited human beings in their perspective on life, but who had practiced law longer, were able to dictate to me about practicing law and also lecture me, without rebuttal, in offhanded manners about my life. It restricted my freedom. I tried to ignore the comments about women, the stereotypes about race, the outright lies, but it built up after a while. It built up to a point where it was hard for that part of me that always seemed to be looking for a fight, to ignore. I was realizing that due to the constraints of time, my life had come to revolve around these people. I had been searching in vain for an outlet from the continual venting of their insecurity of which I felt I was the recipient. Like a conscious Sisyphus, I knew the rock of my contentment would always roll back down the hill. That was life. But I was distraught to discover that there are people in life who, to deflect their own self doubts, want to taunt me as I roll the rock back up the hill.

It was one of those days to escape the world of those who have orgasmic rushes from their moments of apparent domination over another human being. I drank the remainder of the wine from my glass. I needed to piss, but instead of heading for the bathroom, I got up, opened the screen door and stood on the threshold. The rain splattered from the concrete landing onto my feet and shins. I looked around at my neighbors' houses and saw no-one. I pissed out the back door onto the concrete steps. The rain quickly washed it away. It felt good.

THIRTY-FOUR

~

I listened to what he was saying. After all, he was a friend of mine. He had been married for 12 years and, he maintained, had been faithful to his wife the entire time. It was difficult on occasion, but he was able to do it. I tried to look interested. I was concerned that my apathy might be apparent. I leaned on the table and rested my chin, childlike, in the palm of my hand. It was lunch time at Frankie & Johnny's and Penfield had called to meet me for lunch. We were both working, so each of us had on a suit and tie. We were overdressed for Frankie & Johnny's. However, Penfield was in from Atlanta and asked to eat at a good seafood restaurant. I suggested Frankie & Johnny's because the seafood was good and the atmosphere unpretentious. It was a typical New Orleans neighborhood restaurant.

Monogamy was not something that I had spent any amount of time worrying about on the rare occasions that I consented to such an arrangement in a relationship. It had never been inordinately difficult to maintain. Of course, I had only stayed in one relationship for more than four months and that was with Rebekah.

My friend, as I knew he would, again referred to his fidelity during his marriage. He was offering me his advice and the reference was clearly designed to underscore his integrity and convince me of the righteousness of his advice. I wondered momentarily what Caroline would think about someone who trumpeted his compliance with his own promise as deserving of added respect. "It's nothing more than doing what you are supposed to do," I imagined her saying. In that moment, I again realized that centuries of religious beliefs and religious proclamations had not altered the fact that people were rarely willing to be responsible for their actions. Rather, people preferred to subscribe their errors to something immutable and beyond their control, like "evil," or even the catch all excuse: "human nature."

"Anyway," he said, "your problem is that you are always getting involved with these bohemian-types. I mean Rebekah was a beautiful woman, don't get me wrong, but she doesn't have a clue about making relationships work in the real world."

I did not agree with his perspective on Rebekah. I could not actually recall how many times he had even been around Rebekah. He knew nothing about my own issues with relationships. Nevertheless, I nodded my head as if I understood the deeper meaning he was trying to convey. The waitress arrived with our onion rings and the rest of our meal.

He continued to talk while I listened only intermittently. I salted the onion rings and began to eat.

"The thing is," he said, "all women have a chicken little complex. That is, women need to be told every week or so that the sky is not falling. You need to learn to accept that fact," he said. "They will never see the real world like you do." Penfield stopped talking and began to eat.

Unlike my friend, my perspective on the ending of the relationship was a bit different. I knew that I would shut down emotionally at times which made it extremely difficult on Rebekah. I knew that I shut down whenever I felt threatened in any way, when I feared being hurt. It was a mechanism to not allow myself to be hurt. Whenever my instincts picked up that possibility, my system shut down and I resorted to my prisoner mind set. But I also found that I shut my emotions off at other times when there was no discernible threat. I was not certain, but, perhaps, shutting down was my substitute for any emotional response at all. For some reason, I feared a display of any emotions.

However, I was slowly beginning to understand that there was a part of me which assumed that all relationships were a trap, designed to strip me of my freedom, wear down my edges, choke me and reform me into a more acceptable image. I did not really believe relationships were a trap, but I carried the notion with me in some deeper spiritual way. It was probably grounded in some fashion in my father's perspective on his relationship with my mother, or how I experienced it, but I had not fleshed out the components in any greater detail.

I thought about disclosing these thoughts to Penfield but chose not to do so. Some friendships can dive deep and return to the surface as necessary, like an engine that always starts after sitting idle for months. But many remain one dimensional, only skin deep, at the level of laughter at a retold joke. Instead, after a while we began to talk about work. I realized when I decided not to discuss my thoughts with Penfield that I began thinking of the discussion I would have with Caroline about it. My thoughts were not over whether I would discuss it with her, that was a given. Rather my thoughts were like an imagined point-counterpoint over what I would say, how I imagined she would respond and how I would respond. I was working through the sequence, setting out my argument, to be prepared.

After lunch Penfield and I parted. I had a few more hours of work at the office and then I would head home. I was tired and needed some restful sleep.

THIRTY-FIVE

~

I awoke quickly in the middle of the night, with a sudden-ness that left me confused as to where I was. My hands were wet. I pressed my fingers to the palms and felt the moisture. I sat up in bed and realized I had dampness on my neck and chest. I had been dreaming and sweating. My sens-es finally caught up and registered everything around me. I recalled vividly the dream I had just had and my reason for awakening. I felt a slight chill on my back and instinctively pulled my covers around me for warmth.

I had dreamed that I was in a dark green pirogue on a small river, the kind I often fished in as a teenager. The waterway was lined with large moss covered cypress trees. The familiar knees of the trees stood yards in front of the tree line rising, like headless bodies, slightly above the water. I was drifting downstream, alone in the pirogue, except for a small print pillow, a child's pillow, in the bottom of the pirogue. I thought for a moment as I sat in bed, but could not remember how the pillow got into the pirogue. I suddenly remembered, as I recalled the dream, that a picture had hung on the wall above my bed as a child. It was a picture of a large smiling angel, greenish yellow, hovering over, and guarding two children walking across an old worn footbridge.

As I sat in the darkness of my bedroom, my mind re-turned rapidly to the dream. It was a primitive dream without the clear boundaries between being awake and asleep. I was drifting downstream alone when my father had suddenly appeared, with his back to me, seated in front of me in the pirogue. He had a paddle and, without asking me, began maneuvering the pirogue toward the shore. We did not speak as he paddled. Upon reaching the shore he got out of the pirogue and walked away from me toward a large white columned house which sat on the horizon. He had the paddle in his hand and the child's pillow. He did not turn back to look at me or speak as he walked away.

I began to drift down the river again, alone. On the banks of the river I saw a small pier, in disrepair, and a deteriorating clapboard building next to it. A woman stood on the pier dressed in a blue cotton dress. She had on a kitchen apron and had a quilt over her shoulder. I recognized her slowly, as if she was someone I had not seen in a long while. It was Caroline.

She spoke to me, but I could not hear her. I saw her lips move, but I still could not hear her. I thought I could not hear her because of the distance between us, but suddenly I realized I could not hear at all. I could not hear anything. I was deaf.

I looked down into the pirogue for a paddle to maneuver to shore and suddenly noticed I had no legs. I was seated on a plank in the pirogue but had no legs. My pants legs hung neatly from my torso area but were empty. Two black dress shoes, like those I wore to work, were set precisely in the bottom of the pirogue at the ends of my pants' legs. Caroline gestured with her arm for me to steer the boat toward her, but I could not. I then realized that I had no arms. I was seated in the pirogue, but had no arms and no legs and no means of steering the pirogue to where Caroline stood. I could not reach her and she could not reach me.

I saw Caroline jump from the pier into the water as my pirogue began to drift with the current, past the pier. Her cotton dress and the quilt became quickly water soaked. She began to struggle, calmly, to stay afloat in the water, then she bobbed up above the water line almost to her waist as if a spring had momentarily lifted her up before sinking again. The pirogue continued to drift. I could tell that she would not make it to the pirogue. I felt concern that she was going to drown. She looked at me without fear. She was at peace. She mouthed the words: "This is love." She began to sink further beneath the water's surface. I saw her face under the water, her hair still momentarily afloat and spread out on top of the water around her head. I felt cold and afraid. I knew that she was drowning. I tried to move towards her and fell face forward in the pirogue. I felt my face in the dirt and water which had accumulated in the bottom of the pirogue. I could only turn my face slightly out of the water. My torso was stuck. I screamed a silent scream and felt the water and dirt run into my mouth. It was at that moment that I had awakened.

THIRTY-SIX

~

Caroline had an idea. It was supposed to help me figure out what had happened to me during my childhood. It would require the unwitting help of my mother. I hesitated for several days but finally called her to set it all in motion. My mother didn't understand why I had made the request but, seeking to cooperate, she complied.

So on a Sunday morning I reluctantly stopped by my parents' house and retrieved a large box from their front porch containing some of the family photograph albums. The four albums in the box covered the years 1957 – 1968, the first eleven years of my life, or so the binders indicated. I brought them to my house but did not open them. I originally left them stacked on an old church pew which was in my kitchen. Late that afternoon, after waking from a nap, I put a Gatemouth Brown album on the turntable and, as the first song began, I brought the photograph albums to the sofa.

I thumbed through each rather quickly. There were black and white photographs and one or two faded color photographs. There were pictures of my parents when they were young. There were pictures of my deceased sister. Nothing stood out so I went into the kitchen and got a beer. I found a rock glass and filled it up, then returned to the sofa. The coldness of the beer felt good in my mouth. I set the beer down on my end table and then opened up a second picture album. There was a picture of me, my brother and several other children at a party. The

photograph was in color. I took it out of the yellowed four corners that held it in place. On the back of the picture was a date:
"October 30, 1963." October 30th was my birth date. I would
have been six years old on that date. I looked at the picture
again. It was on the back patio of the second house I grew up
in. There were two other pictures that appeared to be taken on
the same day in the album. I was in neither, but my brother
and several of the other children were in those pictures.

I studied the birthday picture with me in it again for a long
time. Something was wrong. The other children in the picture
were all smiling or laughing. There were those childhood gig-
gling faces enjoying the day. Each child had a multi colored
party hat fastened to their head. My mother was leaning over
a child and was cutting a slice of cake on the plate in front of
him with a fork. My six year old face, in contrast to the other
children, was without hint of emotion. There was no smile.
There was no joy at all in my face, as if I did not want to be
there. I tried to recall what must have been my sixth birthday
party. Nothing stirred. My memory was blank. I had no recollection of that party, or any other of my childhood.

Without realizing my purpose, I began to systematically go
through each album and remove the pictures of me. There were
baby pictures, pictures in diapers, school pictures. I removed
each and set them aside in a stack. I was not sure what drove
me to do it, but I was following some evolutionary self preser-
vation instinct.

After I had gone through all the photo albums I leaned
back on the sofa and reached over and took a long sip of my
beer. There, placed on my wooden coffee table, was the photo-
graphic memory of my childhood in two inches of Polaroid's.
There was, perhaps, 15 pictures of me in the photo albums.
Was there any significance to the number? Was it too few?
Did the pictures show anything? There must be more pictures

elsewhere I thought. I recalled nothing in any of the pictures, no event captured or moments in time. I had not noticed any pictures where I appeared injured or bruised. My mind had already made a mental note of that when I was removing the pictures from the photo albums.

Again without precisely understanding my motive I turned each picture over to determine the date and began to put the pictures in chronological order. I spread them out on the floor: 1957 to 1968. All in all, 11 years took up only a small amount of floor space. There was a knock at the door and I got up, grabbed my beer and went to open it.

Caroline was standing on the front porch. I hugged her, let her in, and asked if she wanted anything to drink. She noticed the pictures spread out on the floor.

"Are those your baby pictures," she asked, walking with me toward the kitchen.

"Yes. Everything," I said. I poured Caroline some iced tea.

"Is this the new Gatemouth Brown album?" she asked. I explained that it was an older album that had been re-released. "I like it. Sounds like swing music you could dance to," she opined.

We moved back into the living room quietly. Caroline set her tea down on the coffee table. She removed her sandals and sat cross-legged on the floor.

"Are these in any kind of order?" she asked, looking at the pictures. I explained that I had tried to put them in chronological order. She looked at them for a while. She picked up a few pictures to look at them more closely. My mind was fixated on the picture of me at my sixth birthday party. I referred Caroline to it.

"Why would I look so unhappy at my own birthday party?" I asked. But Caroline seemed distracted. She was focused on something else. She got off the sofa and walked, paced, around and looking hard, examined each picture individually and then in sequence. I started to ask her what she was doing, but she interrupted me.

"Wait," she said abruptly, in focused concentration, tucking her hair behind her ears. I sat with the birthday picture in my hand watching her.

I drank some more of my beer as the Gatemouth Brown album ended. While Caroline continued to look at the pictures I kneeled in front of the stereo and thumbed through my albums. I put a Jeff Lorber album on the turntable.

"Give me your birthday picture," Caroline said, in a voice that commanded me to comply. I handed it to her and she placed it back in the chronology. She then sat back on the floor with her legs beneath her in confirmation, her hands in her lap.

"O.K. Now look at this," she said. I moved closer to her on the floor and in front of the pictures, which were neatly arranged. "In all the early pictures, the black and white ones, you are happy or smiling." I looked at the pictures of me as a very young child. It was indeed a happy face, unfamiliar to me, seeking approbation, but one that I only knew from the photographs.

"But once you turn six, the birthday party picture, you have been looking at, there are no more pictures of you smiling. None between six and eleven years of age," she said. "Look yourself," she said, after a pause for emphasis.

I looked at the pictures and tried to feel something. The child of four and five did look excited and happy, without struggle. Each of those pictures contained wide devilish smiles designed to please a parent, to test how to get approval. The six year old, on the other hand, looked sleepless, somber, emotionally distant, and perhaps, even frightened. As I looked down the row of pictures not a single one after my sixth birthday showed a smile. She was correct. In each of the pictures of me, after six years of age, I looked out vacantly, emptied of emotion. Again I had no spark of recognition from any of the pictures. I still could not recall being in any of the pictures, or any of the events captured by the pictures. My own face, in each picture, was alien to me.

I moved away from the pictures and sat back on the sofa for a moment. I became conscious that my emotional system was shutting down.

"Caroline, I'm not sure I can do this," I mumbled awkwardly. Caroline looked at me expectantly, as she sat on the floor. I grabbed my glass of beer and drank the remainder. I was conscious only of my physical movements. I laughed oddly, a laugh I did not recognize.

"What do you think?" Caroline asked, purposely ignoring my stated reticence. I paused for a moment considering whether to move forward, exhaled before answering and nervously rolled my empty glass in my hand.

"I just don't know that you can read much into ten or fifteen photographs over eleven years. There must be other pictures," I finally said blandly, my voice trailing off. Caroline straightened up.

"Tusa, you have no memory of these years. None," she said, somewhat sternly, taking control and calling me by my last name as she always did. "This is just a starting place. You can't walk away from this." She then hesitated. "But it is striking to me," she said, studying my face to determine how far to push me. "Something happened that has blocked your memory and from these pictures I am guessing it happened, or started, around five or six years of age." I struggled to stay in the moment with her and not retreat behind a wall of denial.

"I just don't know," I said again, disjointed. Caroline sat quietly, looking at me, and then began to pick up the photographs. I got off the sofa and helped her.

"Just think about it," she implored. After sitting with me awhile, reminding me she had a movie she wanted us to see, she left to go to church.

THIRTY-SEVEN

~

S o, how are you doing since Rebekah left and with all the childhood stuff now coming up?" Caroline asked. "I'm all right," I said, feigning confidence, a skill I had long ago mastered. "I've just got to get used to living alone again." I opened the front door to the house all the way, allowing Caroline to walk into the living room. She walked over to the sofa and stood until I gestured for her to sit. She was wearing a purple halter top and low rider blue jeans. I noticed that her hair was pulled back in a ponytail. Caroline had stopped by to pick me up. I had promised to go to a movie with her. I generally did not go to movies. My sense was that anything that gained commercial success was not worth watching, another of my espoused protest principles. However, "Black Orpheus" was playing at the Prytania Theater and Caroline said that I would enjoy it.

"It will get easier," I said. "At the moment, I'm sometimes numb about ending the relationship. What is puzzling, however, is that I just don't completely understand why I brought this relationship to an end. I started to feel trapped as usual, but I can't explain why."

"Is feeling trapped due to the possibility of having to show emotions?"

"I don't know about that. I'd have to think about it."

"Maybe it's part of the kid stuff. Part of whatever happened to you that makes you fear relationships."

"Well, I'm not sure anything happened to me," I demurred.

"Come on Tusa. You know better than that. Don't live in denial. It's not normal to be unable to remember any of your childhood."

"I just don't know," I replied, recognizing that something was stirring inside me that was new and unusual. I could not tell if it was anger or rage, but I feared it.

"What about Rebekah then? Do you want the relationship with her to continue?" Caroline asked, as I moved next to her on the sofa.

"I don't think that I do. I am actually contented at certain times to be back by myself again. It's simpler. And maybe it will give me space to sort out these other things," I said.

"You can't deal with relationship issues unless you are actually in one," she said.

"Nice, Professor Freud," I replied.

"Well, you don't have a lot of faith in relationships, perhaps you should start by trying to figure out why that is so," she said instructively. "If you can get a grip on that issue, it may help you understand your actions. But I'm guessing the link is to your childhood," she concluded. We sat in a brief embrace of silence, as true friends often do. I did not need to immediately reply.

"I have tried off and on for years to figure that one out, but I'm not any closer to an answer. But it seems more difficult this time, more difficult to contain something. It just won't go away," I said. I finally moved to get up from the sofa. Caroline remained seated.

"Presumably, you should start by looking at the principal relationships in your life when you were young, including the one between your parents and between you and your parents," Caroline said, as she repositioned herself comfortably on the sofa. "Maybe something happened in the relationship between you and your parents that affected you in a negative way," she said instructively. "Those pictures we looked at suggest as much," she concluded. She motioned for me to sit back down.

"That's tough, considering I don't remember the first ten or eleven years of my life. In general terms, however, I am certain the relationship with my parents was not good, but it's hard to be specific," I answered.

"What about once you remember? How were you treated then?" she asked. I paused before answering.

"Not too good," I said. "I was run out of the house by my father and recall being put down a lot. I have understood with the passage of time that it was not a supportive environment for me and, perhaps, my folks took out their relationship problems on me," I responded. "But I'm not sure. It's hard to know or have the distance from it to understand such things when you are a kid."

"Why do you think that they belittled you?" she asked, as she repositioned herself again on the sofa so as to be facing me.

"I have no specific recollection," I said, as I leaned forward and, without thinking, intertwined my fingers. I heard the sound of a large truck rambling down interstate. "I can only surmise certain things based on hindsight. I think my parents, or more particularly my father, just decided that I was not very bright and systematically set out to toughen me to the failures in life which he expected for me. Maybe he was reliving his own childhood, but in the role of a parent. Or maybe he was preparing me for the disappointments in life that he had experienced," I said.

"That doesn't explain why they threw you out of the house," she said thoughtfully.

"Oh, I don't remember the flash point each time I was thrown out," I replied.

"It happened more than once?" she asked.

"Yeah, three or four times if I remember correctly," I replied.

Caroline's face reflected a growing anguish. I knew that she had a difficult time understanding such treatment of a child by a parent. It was not part of her personal experience. I did not know what to say to soften the facts for her.

"It wasn't a big deal," I finally said. Caroline did not immediately respond. At that point, I recalled distantly the time I was run off by my father on a family vacation in South Dakota, that I did not want to go on, for reasons I can no longer recall. I had wandered down a highway for an hour or so only to return to the campsite to find my family, apparently unconcerned, around a picnic table eating. I did not relay the story to Caroline.

"What can you recall about your parents' relationship?" she finally asked again.

"That's difficult for me to answer," I said honestly. "I don't recall any fights between them of any substance, but I also don't recall any real affection between them. I think it was mere co-existence," I said. "I don't, however, have a strong impression of them as a couple. I do recall that my father did not think my mother was capable of much outside the home. I think over time he thought his marriage was a mistake and that it had limited him in some ways that he blamed on my mother."

"How do you know that?" Caroline asked.

"Well he told me such things," I replied. Caroline looked at her watch. Apparently we had plenty of time before we had to leave for the movie.

"That's not very healthy for one parent to talk poorly about the other parent in front of their kids," Caroline responded. "It poisons the well. And maybe that's where the idea of relationships as a trap comes from."

I nodded my head slightly in agreement. It had taken me a long time to understand that some of my hostility toward my mother had actually been generated by my father, a suggestion I picked up from a prior girlfriend who was deep in the well of her own therapy. Perhaps he needed that division, to be the chosen parent, another remnant of the demons of his abused and neglected childhood. I did not realize at the time, or for many years after, how easy it was for me to pick up, as an adolescent, on a subconscious level, my father's negative remarks about my mother. Over time the negative view of her grew to such an extent with me that I was unaware of its origin. I just assumed, when I was young, that the perceptions I had of her were my own, or were based solely on her actions. But, perhaps, it was just part of the story I was told by my father.

I confided these points to Caroline, as best I understood that history. She mentioned that the oddity of realizing as a child that my parents' relationship was not what they had pretended it to be, may have caused me to doubt the sincerity of people in all relationships.

"It would certainly leave you with the impression that relationships are phony," she said. I agreed that this was a possibility and immediately thought of Salinger's character Holden Caulfield when she used the word "phony." Maybe that was my attachment to the book? It put in words what I, as an adolescent, could not articulate, about relationships and people, including my own parents. After talking for another twenty minutes or so, and Caroline indicating she was worried about me, we left for the movie.

THIRTY-EIGHT

~

It was a ponytail-earring high-top red converse tennis shoe night out. Her spandex type black dress was cut about six inches above her knees. She had perfectly shaped and tanned calves. The dress had silver buttons running up the front, the first two of which were solicitously unbuttoned. She wore the dress off her shoulder. She was a drop-dead blonde. She was a Hollywood starlet. She was the woman who sat down next to me at the bar at midnight. I had been drinking gin for four hours.

At that point in the evening, and considering the short period of time since Rebekah's leaving, I was in search of a woman who would ask for no proof that I was human. As Danny O'Keefe had sung in a song, "a perfect woman with straight teeth and no last name." My mind was blank to the intricacies of social courtship, to the rules of extended barroom foreplay. I thought of none of these things. My state of mind was the result of Rebekah's leaving, the lurking ghost of my childhood, my drinking, and the exhaustive pressures of work. I had reached the top of the rebellion curve. I had lost the thread of my daily routine. I had always energized myself from within, by withdrawing from people. My internal scenery, however, was now barren. I looked hard at the Hollywood starlet.

She turned in her chair toward me as a result of something I said, the bait in the water. Her right foot brushed intentionally, seductively, against my leg as she turned.

"I'm so sorry," she said softly, with a late night atten-
tive smile.

She was from somewhere in Texas. I heard her say that
she had recently returned to graduate school after ten years
and was working part-time as a waitress to "pay the bills." She
raised her eyebrow in an exaggerated fashion as she said it, as if
to convey a deeper existential meaning, and to let me know that
she was a capable of so much more. I nodded slowly as if I, and
I alone, understood the secret she sought to convey. She was
visiting a married sister in New Orleans whose husband was a
doctor. They had stayed in for the night, but she wanted to see
the nightlife in New Orleans. I imagined what she might look
like undressed. I knew that we would spend the night together.
I had a flash in my mind that we would have sex on the living
room floor of my house.

The Hollywood starlet became suddenly somber and looked
past me. Her mouth turned down with the now noticeable
creases of her age. I realized belatedly that there was a hand
softly resting on my shoulder. I turned and saw that Caroline
was behind me. She walked into the bar behind me without
me having seen her. Her eyes were a bit red and she looked as
if she had been crying. She did not speak, but instead put her
arms around my neck and placed her head on my right shoulder. I pulled her to me gently and put my arms around her tiny
waist. I said nothing. I could not tell if she was crying on my
shoulder, or just resting her head.

With Caroline's head still on my shoulder and my arms
around her, I turned and looked back at the woman with
whom I had been talking. She seemed uncomfortable. I noticed
brown roots in her hair. She wore too much eye liner. I was
embarrassed for her. She was an awkward adolescent trying to
become a member of a high school club that did not want her
membership. It was if she had been caught in a lie, found out

as a fraud, before escaping the sunrise. There would be no walk of shame in the morning.

I grabbed Caroline's hand and turning away from the blonde, directed Caroline to the seat on the other side of me. She sat down and held my hand in her lap.

"What's wrong?" I asked quietly.

She hesitated and as she raised her head to look into my eyes, searching, her eyes welled up with tears. I held both of her hands in mine and gently squeezed them, as she had so often done over the years we had known each other to convey her affection to me. I waited for her to say something and tried to concentrate. She regained her composure, a little.

"I was sleeping . . . and I had a dream about you." A tear gently rolled down the right cheek of her face. Another tear followed shortly thereafter on the left side. Her lips were pursed tightly together to hold her trembling self in check. I let go of her hands for a moment, placed her face gently in my palms and wiped the tears off her cheeks with my thumbs. I struggled to focus on Caroline and block out my surroundings.

"Well, I can see how a dream about me would be frightening," I said, with my hands still on her face, in an attempt to lighten the moment.

"I dreamed that you died," she said, looking away from me and down at her hands. I moved my hands from her face and put her hands back in mine.

"How, if I may ask?" After I asked the question I realized it might not be the best question to ask considering Caroline's apparent emotional state.

"You committed suicide," she said, as her voice broke. She looked hard again into my eyes for some sign of emotion. My demeanor did not change. I wanted to be supportive. I let her words sit temporarily unanswered. She seemed to relax. The tears had stopped.

"Well, just a dream. No big deal," I finally replied, knowing that Caroline genuinely cared about me and that she had a semi-superstitious penchant, despite her Christianity, for reading things into her dreams. Nevertheless, I thought it best to make light of the significance of the dream.

"With you drinking and all this childhood stuff coming up, I'm worried that it might come true," she said, more composed, as she rubbed her eyes with her hands.

I waited a moment and then assured her that while I believed in an individual's right to take their own life, I had no intention of taking my own anytime soon. Caroline did not seem reassured. In that instance, I suddenly recalled my own dream a few nights before of Caroline drowning. I decided not to mention it to her.

I then called the bartender over and ordered cranberry juice for Caroline and a cup of coffee for me. Caroline, with great empathy, told me she was glad that I had not ordered myself any more alcohol. As the drinks arrived, I turned to face the bar and noticed that the blonde had left. Caroline and I sat quietly, for the duration of a juke box song, drinking our drinks. She sniffled on occasion, but had stopped crying.

"Let me clarify something," I said, quietly, as I placed my coffee cup back on the bar. "While I believe in my right to commit suicide, I also believe that Camus was essentially correct that we should not commit suicide out of despair." I ran my hand through my hair scratching at my scalp.

"That's contradictory," Caroline replied, shifting her weight on the bar stool. "And besides, who cares what Camus said." I felt a slight breeze from the front door of the bar as some people opened the door and came in. I turned to look briefly, but did not recognize anyone.

"Well, I care what he said, not because Camus said it, but because it defines a point of reference for me," I replied. I was not sure that Caroline understood my need for such reference points. She waited patiently for a more detailed response.

"In any event, I believe I should have the right to commit suicide, but I don't believe I would exercise it unless I was no longer able to take care of myself," I concluded. I lifted the coffee cup and took a short harsh swallow of the black New Orleans Chicory coffee.

"So you are never going to commit suicide?" Caroline asked hopefully. It was an important question for her. She seemed a little more relaxed now. Part of me wanted to say what I knew she wanted to hear, but I could not. Something in me felt I had to stay unadulterated, like my black coffee, my own form of dogmatism.

"Look, you know this. I don't value my life like so many people seem to value their own these days. I have an 18th century view of life and death, or maybe it's an Eastern one. I can't say that I will never commit suicide, but I have no current plans to do so," I finally responded.

"That's not terribly reassuring," Caroline replied.

"Well, it is my life Caroline and I certainly have the right to do with it what I will," I responded. "I realize that organized religion opposes suicide, but that's only because it is viewed as the ultimate insult to the creator which those religions revolve around," I said.

"I don't know that I agree with the organized religion comment," Caroline said. "But how do you factor in the hurt and pain your suicide will cause to those closest to you?" The conversation was turning away from Caroline's emotions to a more analytical tone, my default position. I was happy with that change as it appeared that Caroline was calmer. If I could convert an issue to its analytical components, I was in more comfortable surroundings.

My initial reaction to her comment about factoring in the feelings of others was to say that there aren't many people who will suffer from my death. I was still feeling a bit numb from all the gin I had drank and frankly had trouble envisioning my death. Like my childhood my possible death seemed remote to me. I could not feel it in any real sense and I attached no significance to the thought of it. However, I was aware that some friends would feel pain if I died, at least I was aware of it in an abstract way. I was certainly aware that it would affect Caroline.

"I'm not sure you will find it satisfactory, but I don't believe that the possible pain of others would affect my decision," I finally replied.

"That's pretty insensitive," Caroline said, after swallowing some cranberry juice.

"I'm not completely comfortable with it from all perspectives, but as far as my right to commit suicide, the feelings of others are not relevant," I answered. In the background, I heard the first notes of Traffic's *Low Spark of High Heeled Boys* on the jukebox. I paused to listen having never understood the meaning of the lyrics. Caroline looked away from me for a moment.

"Let me turn it around," I continued. "If you believed, for example, that the only way you could gain admittance to heaven is if you became, let's say, a Pentecostal--should you become a Pentecostal?"

"Obviously, if I accept your facts, I should," she replied, now facing me again. Her face looked bright. I saw no traces of the fear and concern of a few minutes ago.

"Well, what if your family were all Jewish and opposed your becoming Pentecostal?" I asked her. Caroline paused for a moment and then answered.

"I would certainly weigh their concerns."

"No, you wouldn't," I replied loudly, pointing my finger affectionately at her and leaning toward her. "Because under my facts, you are going to hell if you don't become a Pentecostal."

"I'm not sure I follow the analogy that you are trying to create between the right to suicide and the right to religious choice," Caroline mused. She furrowed her broad forehead in an almost exaggerated fashion. I saw the wrinkles in her olive complexion and they looked out of place.

"Well, both are decisions that should be unaffected by family pressures because the two decisions are probably the most intimate decisions we make," I replied. "Both decisions are made in the heart," I said. The juke box was unplugged and the band was slowly making its way back onto the stage. I heard a woman's laughter from behind me.

"Under your religious choice hypothesis, I can at least try to convince my family why the decision is important to me, I can try to convince them of the value of my choice. As to suicide, there is no flexibility, no dialogue," Caroline replied to me. She stood up and smoothed the front of her dress which I noticed had yellow butterflies on it.

"I am still free to try and convince them about my right to commit suicide. I simply must do it before I commit the act. There is no difference," I responded. The band slowly began its next set with a song I did not recognize.

"I don't buy that," Caroline interrupted, standing in front of me and leaning close to my ear so as to be heard. She put her arm around my shoulder and her lips close to my ear. "One decision retains some flexibility, whereas the other does not," she said. I turned to face her and stood up. I held her in a mild embrace and she draped both arms around my neck, as if she was my partner at the beginning of a Cajun waltz.

"You are worried about the finality of the suicide decision, whereas you think you can change your mind about the religious choice," I whispered in her ear, as we swayed a little in a private absent-minded dance that had nothing to do with the musical beat being played by the band. "But from the standpoint of my right to choose, I believe both rights are absolute," I said

There was a pause in the conversation as we both leaned on each other in dance. She then stopped, leaned her body back and placed her hands on my face to look at me.

"So, are you satisfied that I won't commit suicide?" I finally asked, looking directly into her eyes.

Caroline stared at me. She did not answer me and lowered her head back onto my shoulder.

"Are we still on for dinner with my brother this weekend?" I asked. Caroline kept her head on my shoulder and nodded.

"Looking forward to it," she mumbled.

THIRTY-NINE

~

I remember one summer you had wanted to go to some art camp. I think it was a one-day class. One of those ones that used to be advertised in the TV Guide," he said, in a slightly animated fashion, as if he had been waiting for some time to tell this particular story to me. "Dad had told you that you could not go. He wouldn't pay for it. You kept badgering him and ended up getting punished over it," he continued. I listened closely, but somewhat disinterested. "Anyway, without telling him, you filled out the enrollment form for the art camp and sent it in. Since the camp was not until late August, you figured you could earn the tuition by then and he would never learn about it. I think you planned to catch the Veterans Street bus to go," he said. I continued to listen, but felt as if I was far away. I saw Caroline next to me, watching me.

My younger brother Nicholas looked away from me to Caroline for a moment. I had introduced them earlier that evening and after a couple of drinks over dinner at Palmers, a Jamaican restaurant, she had asked him about our growing up together. In doing so I knew that she was prodding me to learn more about my childhood. He had responded, in part, with this story.

My brother did not look like me. He was darker and looked like my father. I favored my mother in complexion, but was told I looked like my namesake, my great grandfather, when he was younger. Inexplicably, when I think about it, my brother and I were not close. We saw each other infrequently and had very little in common. He had married the only girl he ever dated.

"I still remember the tuition was $30.00, which was a lot of money to us - hell, you were only ten. Anyway, he figured out," my brother said, pointing to me as I tried to focus on what he was saying, "that if he could save money every week he could get the tuition or fee into the camp on time. So he began cutting grass, cleaning garages for neighbors, you name it."

"I thought you were allergic to grass pollen?" Caroline interrupted to ask me. She was seated next to me at the table and across from Nicholas. We had finished our meals and while Nicholas drank water with lemon Caroline and I were drinking Red Stripe beer.

"I am," I replied, without thinking.

"It was terrible for him in those days," my brother volunteered. "He would cut people's grass with a red bandanna tied around his face like a bank robber and tuck the bottom of the bandanna into the neck of his tee-shirt. He told me it was his air filtering system." My brother chuckled and then lifted his glass of water to drink. Caroline and I sat quiet.

"Well, believe it or not, he earned enough to go and again without Dad knowing, he mailed in the $30.00 in cash," my brother said, with his elbows on the table. It was hard to tell if he simply enjoyed telling the story or if, rather, he admired the fact that I had accumulated the money. Caroline raised her beer bottle and took a sip.

"You see," I interrupted quietly, to confirm my lack of a childhood memory, "I have no recollection of going to an art camp--"

"--You didn't go," my brother interrupted me. There was quiet at the table as if no-one was sure how to proceed.

"What do you mean?" Caroline finally asked, as I grew uneasy for no reason which I could identify. My brother had a disquieting laughter in his voice, and stared away from me and directly at his hands on the table.

"Dad wouldn't let you go." He paused and his uneasiness was visible on his face, a face recalling a past trauma.

"When dad found out what you had done, and he found out when the art camp sent you an acknowledgment letter, he called you into the kitchen, tore the letter up in front of you and told you that you were not going." My brother relayed this in a tone of hard-edged laughter, reserved for the bitter and the elderly, recalling the hard times of their childhood. I strained for any sense of recognition to what I was hearing. All was quiet in my head. "Boy, was he angry when he realized what you had done. You got punished again for your efforts," Nicholas said. My brother looked away from his hands on the table and directly at me for a moment. It was a look of uncertainty and compassion.

"I don't remember any of that," I said, without emotion to Caroline.

My brother with that same type of restrained laughter he had previously displayed, said, "it was the damn acknowledgment letter that got you caught. You had everything else covered, but you were too young to realize that they would write you back to confirm your acceptance."

FORTY

~

C aroline says that you are an atheist," a disembodied voice standing above me said. I was seated at a small table in the corner of the Dante Street Deli where I had arrived alone for an early dinner. I had not yet ordered my meal. I looked up from my legal pad, on which I had been scribbling phrases for a possible future poem, to see Loretta standing next to my table. I was surprised to see her and even more surprised that she was speaking to me after my last regrettable comments to her. Forgetting her question-like comment, I asked her to sit and offered to buy her something to drink. She accepted the invitation to sit at my table with a nervous nod of her head, but declined the offer of a drink by saying she was not thirsty. I glanced around the restaurant at its six or eight tables, but did not see any of her friends.

It was clear that Loretta was looking for someone to talk to about something. She looked a bit uncomfortable. I set my pen and pad to the side of the table

"When did you last see Caroline?" I asked to try and get the conversation going. I noticed that Loretta's hair was neatly trimmed. She had 3 or 4 earrings in each of her ears. She had a small crucifix on a short chain around her neck. I could not describe her as "cute," but did think her attractive.

"I saw her again last week at NOMA, the art museum. We get together every so often and talk. Well, mostly I talk about childhood stuff and Caroline listens," she said. "I am having trouble deciding if she is a very old soul or a very young one. You have known her for a while and I thought you might have some insight on it." The waiter approached my table to see if I was ready to order. I caught his glance and waved him off.

I did not consider Loretta's pondering of the issue with Caroline as odd. I was well aware that Caroline prompted a variety of diverse reactions, including, on occasion, jealousy, from women she met.

I had often heard a friend of mine describe people as "old souls" or "young souls." The concept seemed very Buddhist-like, at least to the extent that it suggested that our spirits or souls continue to return to work out our issues. On a certain intuitive level, I thought I understood the concept, but only in its extremes. I certainly knew individuals whose whole life seemed to be a series of self-inflicted crises, stepping from one pile of shit to another. I generally regarded these individuals as the very young souls, here for their first life. On the other hand, the individuals who dove deeper on issues and were untroubled by them, I considered as the old souls. It was the difference between sight and vision. I was not sure that my conception of the old souls was perfectly correct. It seemed to me that the old souls were supposed to be more ego-less, more accepting and less worried about the world around them. My conception of old souls may have been colored by my own thoughts of where I wished that I fit into the concept.

"I would think it would be easy to tell whether she is an old soul or a young soul," I finally added. "Are you sure you don't want something to drink," I asked again. Loretta shook her head negatively.

Loretta had her hands on the table and the fingers of both hands were intertwined. I sensed she was trying to judge whether she should continue the conversation with me. She had already made the decision to trust me enough to approach me. Now she was hesitant.

"Well, I have often wondered if the really old souls regain their innocence before they disappear for good," she replied. "Caroline has such a wonderful innocence about her that she has forced me to wonder if that is a characteristic of some later stage. I'm certainly more comfortable with that image of her than with her as a very young soul."

I thought briefly that there must be some law of physics that states that everything returns to its original state; perhaps the innocent once again becomes innocent. It then struck me that the Catholic ritual of Ash Wednesday might be symbolically analogous. I mentioned these thoughts in a piecemeal fashion to Loretta.

"Look, I don't believe we have a soul. I think that was simply a pre-modern way to describe our consciousness, what we would today, probably because of Freud, would call the 'self.' But I think I know what you are trying to express about Caroline. I'm not sure I am comfortable with the word 'innocent' even though I have used that phrase myself to describe her," I replied. We both smiled, a shared understanding. "I have often thought of her as pure, or angelic even, but have struggled to put a precise description on it. Words are often inadequate to describe our feelings and that's true when it comes to Caroline. But it's not, I grant you, unlike an aspect of the innocence of childhood before society intervenes and distorts us," I said.

Loretta now glanced around the restaurant as if she was suddenly worried someone might see her with me. The friendly smile she had shared with me disappeared. I did not know whether she was going to abruptly end the conversation or not. I was hoping she would not, perhaps, trying to make up for my prior comments to her the last time we met. She glanced at me.

"So you believe she is an old soul?" Loretta finally asked.

"Must be. From what I understand of the young soul--old soul idea, I can't see how she can be anything else. She is too much at peace with herself to be a young soul," I replied.

"Are you an atheist?" she asked again. I was surprised Caroline had shared this with her and was curious why it mattered to her.

"Yes, I am," I replied.

"The reason I asked is, if you are, that is, is to ask you how people can determine their value system if there is no God? That is a bit inarticulate, but . . . I've often wondered about it in my own life," she said.

"I think I understand the question," I interrupted, rescuing her. Since I had never really had any substantive discussions with Loretta, I did not want to use a tone that might discourage her. I was used to being the bull in the china cabinet in such discussions. Clearly, I also realized that I wanted the conversation with her to continue.

"I am not sure that I can give you a formula on that one, but I can tell you my reasoning as to how I have tried to do it," I said, pausing. "And not all of this was conscious at the beginning." Loretta seemed to be interested and nodded slightly to indicate I should proceed.

"First, I am certain, as my father used to say, that 'the apple does not fall far from the tree.' By that, I mean I was raised a Catholic and consequently, when I rebuilt my value system after making a decision that there is no God, it probably borrows, subconsciously, from that background," I said.

"So, you believe you can actually build your own value system," she stated, as if summarizing my remarks. I could tell, however, that she was not going to be easily convinced.

"I think that you have no alternative," I replied. "I mean, I have two choices. I can simply adopt someone else's structure, whether Buddhist, Existentialist or whatever, or I can construct my own system. If I have gone through the trouble of lifting the boulder to see if anything is really under it and conclude that there is no God, I don't believe I could just adopt someone else's system. That would be a weakness," I replied.

"So is your value system just a revamped Catholicism?" she asked. I sensed that Loretta was relaxing. She placed her elbows on the table and leaning forward placed her chin in her hand. I noticed several rings on her fingers. I relaxed as well. Happy that with all the turmoil in my life I could, in fact, be cordial.

"That's a pejorative way of putting it," I replied. I noticed Loretta lean back slightly increasing the distance between us. "But seriously, I don't think that's correct. I think I have discarded a significant amount of 'Catholic' ideas that I found incongruent and then incorporated my own elements and continually shaped all of it with my own experiences. And that continues, as it must," I said, trying to keep a steady tone.

"Give me an example," she said quickly.

"Well, I don't believe in heaven or hell. I don't believe in any original sin idea . . . ."

"But that's just an outgrowth of your belief that there's no God," she interrupted. "How do those things relate to a value system?" she asked.

"Well, in a larger sense, without the reward or punishment system, it reaffirms my principal ethic and that is threefold: One, that this is the only life I get. No afterlife to redeem me or hold on to. Two, that I have complete free will. Three, that as a result I am completely responsible for my actions or inactions in this life. No external excuses," I replied. "It is the responsibility part which shapes my moral code and assures that I treat people properly, the way I would want to be treated. A Kantian idea, or a Christian idea if you like. By the way, not that I have succeeded, as you are aware," I then said.

"It sounds kind of like Christian atheism, if there is such a thing," Loretta said. I leaned forward in my chair toward her. "Actually there was a developing branch of theology in the 1960's called 'radical theology,' that proposed just such a system," I said calmly. "I do not know that it gained much acceptance with mainstream theology," I stated.

"That's interesting," Loretta said, appearing suddenly distracted. She leaned back completely in her chair and turned her legs outward from the table as if she was going to depart.

"I believe one of the authors' of that theology was a guy named William Hamilton," I offered gratuitously. Loretta pulled a pen out of her knapsack and slowly wrote the name on her hand. I thought about whether I should ask her if she was an atheist, but decided I would not. The waiter approached our table again and simply stood there.

"Is there some reason you are wondering about all of this?" I asked, ignoring the waiter. Loretta slowly moved her chair back from the table and stood up.

"I was just wondering," she said hurriedly, appearing embarrassed in front of the waiter by my question. She then told me she really had to run and asked that I ask Caroline to call her.

"Does she have your number?" I asked.

"Yes," she replied.

I watched Loretta as she walked out of the restaurant. I was unsure of the exact reason she spoke to me. I made a mental note to tell Caroline that Loretta asked about her. The waiter then asked if I wanted to hear about the restaurant's "specials."

FORTY-ONE

~

I ran into Loretta the other day and she asked that you call her," I said, as, hands in my pocket, I looked out the picture window in my living room. It was raining hard outside yet the sun was still occasionally peeking through the clouds. It was the type of rain in New Orleans that was common and intermittent. Caroline raised her eyebrows a bit. An amused look appeared on her face.

"Did she actually speak to you?" I turned away from the window to face Caroline.

"Yes, she did, and I might be wrong but she seemed to be a bit distressed about something. Asked me about my atheism and my value system," I said. I moved slowly away from the window off of a piece of carpet onto the hardwood floor. One of the floor boards creaked as I stepped on it. I stayed standing in front of Caroline with my hands still in the pockets of my shorts.

"Yes, I'm guilty. I told her a bit more about you as she seemed interested. She is always a little stressed out when I see her. She'll probably be a good therapist 'cause she tends to see everything from a psychological perspective," Caroline replied. I smelled a mild fragrance and realized it was perfume. I had not recalled Caroline ever wearing perfume before but, perhaps, I had never noticed.

"I didn't know you saw her that often," I said.

"We get together occasionally. I enjoy the conversations," Caroline said, sounding flat, maybe slightly protective. "She always wants to talk to me." She moved her hips in the chair in which she was seated as if her dress was uncomfortable. A stray male cat, that I had named Remus, and had been feeding, pushed his way into the house through the partially opened screen door. After cautiously looking around he lay down on the floor at a safe distance and began grooming himself. Caroline tried to call the cat to her. It paused for a second, looked at Caroline without interest, and continued its grooming. "She has had a pretty rough life," Caroline said.

"What do you mean?" I asked. I looked out the picture window again. The rain was coming down harder.

"Well, the little bit I gathered from her was that she left home after being abused by her step father. Her mother is deceased and she has no family. She was married for about a year to a guy who also beat her up quite frequently," Caroline detailed.

"At least that may explain some of her hostility to men," I responded, moving towards the sofa to sit down. My movement startled Remus, who eyed me nervously, as he quickly got up and pushed his way through the screen door back onto the porch.

"I'm not sure she is hostile to men. I think she is just guarded in general," Caroline said.

"Apparently not with you," I replied.

"We've been discussing it. Maybe that's why she talked to you. A first step. Exposure therapy, if you will," Caroline said.

"Glad to know I could be part of her therapy," I said, with a slight laugh. Caroline smiled as well. "She told me," I then said, as I sat down, "that she could not decide if you were a very old soul or a young soul."

Caroline looked at me a little perplexed and pursed her lips together. She moved again in the chair as if still trying to get comfortable. I gave her, as best I understood it, an overview of the old soul-young soul theory. Caroline seemed most interested about the idea of becoming wiser on each return.

"Is that a religious theory?" she asked, amused, but inquiring. She had finally slipped her shoes off and pulled her legs up under her.

"Maybe its tied to the thirty-one planes of existence in some Buddhist thought. But I'm not sure," I replied. Caroline studied on what I had said, but did not respond. I looked out the picture window again and saw part of a rainbow in the distance, as Remus walked back into the room like he owned it.

"And where do you fit? Old soul or young soul?" she asked, bemused.

"I thought you knew," I said.

"Answer, please," Caroline replied.

"I don't have a soul," I said.

FORTY-TWO

~

For reasons that I could not explain, but assumed was precipitated by the recent conversation with my brother over dinner, I began to seize upon and contemplate, in earnest, the fact that I could not remember my childhood. In a matter of days, the contemplation became an obsession that I struggled to blunt. It culminated one morning with me losing my temper with a woman in the grocery store who, in front of me, was hitting her crying child. I confronted her, loudly, standing between her and her child and telling her to "hit me" instead of the kid. I had to be restrained by store personnel as I screamed at her to hit me instead of the child. She became frightened and immediately left the store. I drove home from the store in barely controlled rage. For, perhaps, the first time in my life I wanted to hit someone.

While it seemed on the surface to have built up quickly in importance to me, I was aware that it was an issue I had thought about, from time to time, for many years. The ending of the relationship with Rebekah and my inability to explain it, other than feeling trapped, and Caroline's review of my childhood pictures may also have been part of the breakthrough.

I had to get control of it and so I determined silently to write out a listing of every event from my childhood that I could remember, with the dim hope that such a listing would calm my growing restlessness and prove, perhaps, that I, in fact, had some memory of aspects of my childhood. After two weeks my recollections filled six lines on a page of loose leaf paper. And I was not really sure if those were actual memories, or stories I had heard about me. The strongest memory I had, that came tumbling out in the writing process, was sleeping with the covers over my head at night. I showed it to Caroline without explanation. She seemed to understand immediately.

Caroline asked me if I recalled anything further about the art camp my brother had told us about. I told her I remembered nothing.

"Do you even recall being interested in art, or drawing when you were young?" she had asked, hoping to spark a memory. I had told her that my mother had informed me once that I drew lots of pictures when I was a child and that I had indeed found several of those drawings stored in a box in the attic when I was a teenager. My scrawled childhood signature was on the bottom of each picture, but I had no recollection of drawing any of the pictures. When she asked, I told Caroline that I recalled most of the drawings were of mythical, or science fiction-type creatures.

"I did not draw pictures of humans," I told her.

I was still perplexed by all of this. I could not completely understand why, at this moment in my life, at 34 years old, recalling the first ten or eleven years of my existence had become so urgent. Yet, there was an intensity to my desire to shine light on that dim recollection that had apparently welled up inside of me for years. It now spilled out.

I tried to contain it and understand it. I used every intellectual control technique for corralling and shutting off my emotions that I had developed in a lifetime of control, but I failed. Without warning I found it would completely muddle my focus. It pushed its way past the well guarded gates of my thought process, disarmed my intellectual sentinels, disrupted my concentration and held me hostage demanding in a strange tongue to take stage and be heard. Rage welled up inside of me. I did not know what to do, so I spoke to Caroline about it.

It was an awkward feeling to be so helpless in the face of an emotional response. I had no common language with which to communicate with it.

Caroline stayed with me in the evenings, after work, for a few days because, she said, depression had overtaken me. She had shown up at my door with a few of her belongings and walked in without asking permission, as I opened the door. I was not aware that I was depressed. For the next few days she held witness to my rambling night time discourses, my occasional crying, and hours of complete silence. I recall having extreme difficulty expressing my thoughts to her. Caroline painstakingly pulled isolated words out of me to form sentences. I felt briefly better after each such effort on her part. I can never imagine having allowed anyone else to see me in such a condition. I felt completely safe with her, a feeling that I had never felt with anyone else.

I found myself, periodically and without obvious provocation, in an unrestrained temper that had no direction, no immediate focal point. I began to recognize that it was the prior isolated instances of hostility that had been piling up and was now overwhelming me. I conjured up scenarios in my head where I openly displayed my anger to others over imaginary insults. Even though I realized my anger had come from a fictitious scenario I would still possess the anger for hours after I had dismissed the scenario.

Then as quickly as the rage had overtaken me it gained balance. Though unexplainable to me at the time, its focus was the face of my father. I argued with him. I bested him in imaginary discussions. I berated him for his prior actions. And all of this occurred in my head, making me wonder if I was losing touch with reality. The rage became anger, then hostility

which dissolved into disdain, and finally a mild form of acceptance. Eventually, it left me with some feeling of forgiveness,
for both of us. Perhaps, I thought, this process was necessary,
an emptying of myself, in order for my repressed emotions to
begin to take form. Maybe I needed to first express my anger,
if only to myself, over the years of repression, before I could
develop further emotionally. It was a Gordian knot that I had
to untie in order to be free of the weight of a memory denied.
When lucid enough I had such thoughts and discussed them
with Caroline. She listened patiently.

I slept during that time, but only fitfully. I would retreat to
the kitchen to make hot tea in the dark early morning hours.
On occasion, I would awake to find Caroline laying on her side
of the bed looking at me. Once I awoke and found that she was
no longer in the bed beside me. I got out of bed to look for her
and found her in the living room seated in the dark. When I
turned the lamp on, she had her Bible open in her lap and
tears followed a soft path down her cheeks. She shook her head
negatively and pursed quivering lips when I asked what was
wrong. I don't know how long she had been seated in the dark.

After a few days I told Caroline that I was feeling much
better. She left the house reluctantly and called me every day
for the next four or five days to check on me. I had to promise
not to disconnect the phone and answer it if it rang.

"I have an idea for you to think about," Caroline said to me,
in an upbeat tone on the phone one day shortly after she had
left the house. When I did not immediately respond, Caroline
continued. "Since you have no recollection of your childhood,
perhaps, you should talk to your brother some more and ask
him to tell you more stories about what happened. It might
spark some recollection."

"I don't really see him that often," I replied flatly, in a
monotone deflection.

"So make some time," she responded, expressing her frustration. I agreed that it was something to think about.

"I know you don't want to hear this," she said, prefacing her remarks. Then she paused as if she was not sure whether to say what she was thinking. "God will not put more on you than you can handle," she finally said. "I'm going to ask that you not respond to my last remark, even though you don't believe it. Just use it as a comfort without thinking any further about it. Can you do that?" she asked.

"Only for you," I replied, in acknowledgment of my debt to her. We then agreed to meet for breakfast on the weekend.

FORTY-THREE

～

Then you shall judge yourself,' the king answered. 'That is the most difficult thing of all. It is much more difficult to judge oneself than to judge others. If you succeed in judging yourself rightly, then you are indeed a man of true wisdom.'" Caroline looked up from where she was reading. She looked happy. There was a contentment, a wise acceptance, in her that I always knew was there, but I suddenly noticed it again. I felt peace flow over me as I looked at her.

"I think," she said, "we should judge ourselves today." She then set down the copy of *The Little Prince* which she had brought to breakfast, a copy which I had given her several years before. As she placed the book on the counter top where we were seated, the middle age female proprietor of Liz's Café set down our breakfast in front of us.

Caroline had told me she would bring a quotation for our meeting in the morning. Having frequented Liz's on Metairie Road for the past few months, I was certain that the denizens, even on a Saturday morning, were unaccustomed to conversation that didn't concern football, baseball, or some television show. Nevertheless, I liked the place and felt comfortable there. Liz and the regulars were always friendly to me. It was my favorite place to eat breakfast while I read the morning paper.

I took Caroline's selection of a quotation to reflect her desire for an opportunity for each of us to talk about the issues we felt we were trying to deal with and whether we felt we were succeeding, or failing, with those issues. As we ate I began to try and catalog the issues confronting me on a personal level. I knew that my first issue was my constant need to withdraw and be by myself for days at a time. I would actually feel myself getting physically ill if I did not have time alone. Secondly, I knew that my problems with relationships masked something about me. I generally tired quickly of relationships and I did not understand why. My third issue, perhaps the foundation of the other two, was the growing hostility, an inner anger about the phantom shadow of my childhood.

"Who starts?" I asked, as I reached for the salt shaker on the counter.

"I will," Caroline said, still chewing on some toast. "I am still working on being nonjudgmental about Loretta's lifestyle. I have good days, but on occasion I don't feel I am handling it properly."

I was surprised by Caroline's listing of Loretta's lifestyle as an issue. From my perspective, and from what she had told me, I thought it was a non-issue. She indicated that while she was comfortable around Loretta, she struggled with whether Loretta's lifestyle was immoral, but she wanted to reach her own decision. She indicated that she did not understand biblically why it was immoral, although she was well aware of the reference in Leviticus about it. She said that since the reference was in the Old Testament, as a rule governing a nomadic tribe, she needed to think about it further.

"I'm not a biblical literalist. I think if you are unwilling to wrestle with the biblical text and its meaning then, perhaps, your faith is not really that deep," she said.

"Sounds like Thomas Merton," I replied, recalling my reading of his writings.

I asked her if her decision would affect her developing friendship with Loretta. Caroline said she thought it was unlikely that she would decide Loretta's lifestyle was immoral and, as a result, unlikely it would affect their friendship. It was a typical response from Caroline. She really never passed judgment on anyone, even if it allegedly conflicted with a literal reading of the Bible. In a time where pettiness and dogma dictated most people's approach to life and religious belief, and clouded mine on occasion, Caroline stood apart from the crowd.

I told her she should consider talking to Loretta about it. Caroline indicated she was not ready for such a direct approach. But, she said, it was a possibility after she had thought about it some more.

Caroline ordered some more coffee and then asked me to select an issue I was working on. I told her that I was not making much progress on understanding my need to be alone, to withdraw from social settings.

"It's a problem that I have always had," I told her. "And I still don't have a clue as to its exact origin. Maybe its evolutionary; you know, the wounded animal who hides to protect itself from predators. Actually, my sense is that maybe as a child I was in a situation where I felt the only support I received was internal, from myself. As a result, and this is only a guess, I probably developed a technique of withdrawing so as to reinvigorate myself instead of relying on others."

"If that is true, why is that a negative? Happiness should never be based on what others think of you, or on anything external," Caroline asked.

"Or it may be a learned technique to avoid getting hurt. I'm not sure I can explain it, but I have become increasingly uncomfortable with how often I isolate myself," I replied.

"Perhaps you are just in a period where you are being exposed to more stressors and that results in your needing more time alone," Caroline said. I told her that it was a possibility, but that I still saw it as a long-term problem that I needed to correct.

"Regardless of why I do it, it comes off too often as being anti-social," I said.

"Well, I've seen you do that on occasion, be anti-social. But isn't that more about how you withdraw instead of why you withdraw?" she asked.

"In other words, it's OK to withdraw, just don't be an asshole about it," I paraphrased.

"Exactly!" Caroline giggled, clapping her hands together lightly.

"And this childhood stuff, the loss of memory, is really nagging at me, dampening my spirit," I said.

"It's going to come to the surface again. You can't lock it back up," Caroline cautioned me. I knew she was right, but I still didn't know what to do about it.

We talked for a little longer after finishing our meals, but Liz's had filled up so we gave up our seats at the counter. I walked Caroline to her car and we spoke for a few more minutes. We agreed to call each other during the week and get together again.

FORTY-FOUR

~

As I was driving across the Causeway bridge I found myself composing a eulogy, in my head, for a cousin who was a sort of kindred spirit. I looked out at the waters of Lake Pontchartrain. The lake was polluted and had been posted against swimming for years. Recently the shell dredging in the lake had been stopped and, as a result, the water was finally getting some of its normal color back, like someone awakening from having passed out.

My cousin was still very much alive but I was, for some reason, imagining what I was saying at his funeral. My cousin and I were the only remaining members of the immediate family who were not married. While we had striking dissimilarities---from physical appearance to educational background---we had shared childhood experiences.

I recalled that he used to joke with me about our difficulties with relationships. Something we had in common.

"You know how we know we are in love, cousin?" he would ask, rhetorically. "No," I would reply, already knowing his answer.

"They take us to the hospital bent over in pain," he would then answer with taut laughter.

We were both considered the problem child in our respective families. We were labeled as rebellious. We were drilled with numerous, "Why must you do everything the hard way?" questions from upset and irate parents. We were told we were different. We were cautioned with the physical threat of a beating that "a hard head makes for a soft tail." We were told we were not very bright. We were hounded on a daily basis about our perceived inabilities, we were put in a childhood prison, and, to the complete surprise of our parents, instead of acquiescing and allowing ourselves to be molded, we rebelled.

Our rebellion against our parents was sparked by a spirit that we did not realize existed. Each small act of opposition, or refusal, raised by us to some parental restriction, or rebuke, was our message to them and to ourselves, although we were unaware of it at the time, that our life had more meaning than they were willing to attribute to it. We expressed that meaning in the minor displays of individuality that we were able to muster and that our parents often classified as our "signs of rebellion." Our unkempt hairstyle was proof of that meaning. Our refusal to wear the clothes selected for us was proof of that meaning. Our attachment to a pair of worn out tennis shoes was as well.

The spirit that silently whispered to our subconscious that our life had value could not be killed by abuse. Rather, the more severe our circumstance, the more restrictive our environment, the more steadfast and exaggerated that spirit became in its bold affirmation of the value of our life. It was a spirit which would not be denied and it cost us, sometimes dearly. Now, years later, he and I each struggled to sort out the meanings of those acts we took so long ago and the oppression we suffered as cause and effect. He had moved to Montana, ostensibly for work. I recognized his move as the need for distance between himself and a family structure he found inhospitable, a way to escape too much personal history. He had, in a sense, disappeared as I imagined I would do one day.

I wondered why I would sometimes envision myself at someone's funeral speaking about the person's life. Perhaps it was a ritual that kept me awake to my connection with the person. On the other hand, it may have been a throwback to my mild contemplation of death as an adolescent. Although the memories were not vivid, I recalled that I considered it with some frequency. At the age of 13, behind a locked bathroom door and seated on a clothes hamper, I held my father's loaded 22 derringer in my hands. I sat on the clothes hamper for a long time crying. I held the derringer loosely in my hands and my hands shook. I do not recall what specifically precipitated my contemplation of suicide, what conflict or rejection. I looked at the white ivory handle of the gun in my palm. I looked at myself in the bathroom mirror on several occasions across from the clothes hamper. I got as close as slipping my index finger over the trigger of the gun. The spirit, of which I was unaware, stopped me.

FORTY-FIVE

~

I was drunk again. It was a little past midnight. The front door to the Maple Leaf was open and the humidity from an earlier rain was still thick in the air. I wondered how many nights each year I went out to drink. I made a mental note to consider recording each night out drinking in some code on my calendar at work.

I stood up, adjusted the barstool beneath me and leaned forward, placing my elbows on the bar. It was a slow night and Emily, the bartender, was washing glasses. Loretta had been seated next to me for 20 minutes or so with her back to the bar watching the dancers on the dance floor. I had acknowledged her polite "hello" when she arrived with a simple nod of the head as I lifted my glass. She had not tried to engage me in conversation and I had not volunteered anything. I was tired and lethargic. Perhaps it was from drinking too much. Perhaps I was worn out from carrying the weight of the things I could not figure out.

As the band ended its set, Loretta pivoted on her barstool and faced me. I could see in the mirror behind the bar that her hair was pulled back in a short ponytail and she had a blue handkerchief tied as a bandanna on her head. As usual, she wore no make-up. I assumed that she was wondering if Caroline was going to show up tonight.

"Every time I see you in here you have been here a while," she said, in pleasant, but tentative voice. I smiled slightly, but did not respond. Loretta then volunteered that Caroline was a bit worried that I drank too much. I could imagine Caroline expressing her concern to Loretta about me.

"Well someone said the road of excess makes me wiser," I finally said, purposely unapproachable.

"I doubt you mean to say that getting drunk makes you wiser, or smarter," Loretta said, lecturing. She seemed either unsure of whether to challenge my comment directly, or uninterested in pursuing the discussion. I could not, drunk as I was, tell which it was.

"Are you familiar with William Styron?" I then asked, still not making direct eye contact with her, but watching her in the bar mirror. Loretta nodded her head, but I could not tell if it was in the affirmative or not. "Well, Styron wrote something to the effect that it was alcohol," I said, and paused mid-sentence trying to remember the exact quotation. "It was alcohol which, quote, 'let my mind conceive visions that the unaltered, sober brain has no access to. Alcohol was an invaluable senior partner to my intellect,' unquote," I concluded, happy with my ability to recall the quotation.

Loretta looked at me disapprovingly and without speaking. Her eyes seemed to darken. "And Jimmy Buffett said, 'it makes me quite immobile but it lets my feelings show,'" I added for levity. Loretta then smiled. I did not recall ever seeing her smile at anything I said. I turned to face her and smiled back.

"You need to read Styron's *Darkness Visible*, more closely," she finally said, confidently. "I don't think Styron is saying alcohol promotes intellect or wisdom." She might be right, but I couldn't remember. I was comfortable with the role alcohol played for me. It opened an emotional door, however slight, that I could not open sober. Maybe it loosened some other chains for a while.

She then asked, as if sensing what I was thinking, if I was advocating my alcohol use for intellectual purposes, like I believed Styron did, or for emotional purposes, like Buffett. Somewhat uncertainly, as I had not thought it through, I indicated that it was for both purposes. Again there was a pause in the conversation, a residual lack of comfort with each other.

"You seem to have thought out the reasons for your actions. At least you say you have," Loretta then stated, unaware that I was winging it, but, perhaps, sensing it.

"I hope," I said calmly, "that I have thought about the justifications for all my actions and inactions. That," I continued, "would be consistent with living a conscious life."

"Do you believe that you live such a life?" Loretta asked, as she raised her hand to indicate to Emily that she wanted another glass of water.

"I hope that I do. Because sometimes," I paused, "it is the only goal I can hold onto in life." Loretta now placed her elbows on the bar in a relaxed fashion and looked down at the floor.

"I don't know that I understand what you mean by a 'goal,'" she said. I lifted my glass of gin and swallowed.

"I think sometimes that the only goal I have in my life is to remain conscious of the absurdity around me, the illusions and temporary distractions that people think are real, and never fool myself into believing those illusions about life," I replied. I felt I had not explained that very well. Loretta must have sensed this and did not reply. "I guess I use staying conscious in the same sense that Camus uses it with *The Myth of Sisyphus*," I then stated. "Anyway, in order for me to remain conscious, I must constantly reflect on my life, my actions and inactions and never fool myself into believing there is ultimate meaning in any of my actions. The rock will always roll back down the hill waiting for me."

"The way you describe it makes it sound like you carry it as a burden," she said. I sat for a moment too long and thought about what she said. Maybe, I thought too many things in life were a burden. I wondered why? I could hear through the open front door that a slow rain had started to fall again.

"What's the saying about life, red in tooth and claw?" I replied.

"What about the people who live an unreflective life, the category most people fall into. Are you saying their lives are of less value than yours?" I sipped at the ice remaining in my glass.

"I can't make such value judgments for others," I said, knowing full well that I felt disappointment about such folks. "However, the person who lives an unreflective life, in my mind, makes a bargain with a monster they are unwilling to confront," I said. I started to get animated in my response. "The bargain is that the person agrees not to raise or consider certain uncomfortable issues, to remain comfortably numb, and to live within the walls built by the monster. In exchange, the monster agrees to allow the person to live in ignorant peace within the walls. The monster gets its prisoner and is safe from the prisoner's potential harm by inquiring and the prisoner gets to pretend there is no monster and avoid any harm by confronting the monster."

"And who is the monster?" she asked, curious but doubtful.

"The self," I replied promptly. "The imagined self," I corrected.

Loretta turned her barstool back around and faced the dance floor. She looked away from me toward the dance floor. I wondered if I had revealed too much of myself and at the same time whether I even believed what I had said. The band started the first song of its final set for the evening. Loretta did not respond to my monster story.

FORTY-SIX

~

How was your visit with your uncle? He's still single, right?" the voice on the phone said, when I unexpectedly picked up. It was Caroline. She knew that I had gone to visit my uncle who was dying of cancer in the hospital. In fact, even though she did not know him or my family, she had offered to go with me for support. Although I have never been able to fully explain the discomfort of family gatherings, Caroline had grown to understand, or accept, this part of me. She felt she could help me deal with my distress around family if she was present. In fact, she described herself as a "buffer" when she offered to go. I was never sure what it was about family get-togethers but, on the rare occasions when I was with my family, I was often overcome with a physically suffocating feeling.

Caroline also knew that my Uncle had often sheltered me when, as an adolescent, I had problems at home. He was not really my uncle, but my father's childhood friend that I called my uncle. He was a bear of a man who smoked filter-less Pall Malls and had driven an over the road eighteen wheeler truck all his life. As an adolescent, I found comfort in his physical presence, as if his size alone was sufficient to guarantee me protection. He treated me as an equal, took me to sporting events, out fishing and once asked me to rank his girlfriends that I had met. His sense of humor was as large as he was, telling me often, for example, that he had taught Johnny Unitas how to throw a football and Pete Maravich how to shoot a basketball.

My uncle lived in the small town of Abita Springs. A nice little town surrounded by the burgeoning population of white baby boomers who had fled the city for fear of crime, fear of race and fear of change. They disguised their white flight by hardily claiming that they were "moving to the country." Fear, he taught me, is rarely identified by its purveyors as such. It is usually dressed up and called by another name to make it more palatable. Once arrived, they changed the "country" they claimed to be enamored with into the more familiar suburbs. The scenery in Abita was, however, nice. As to his move to the "country" my uncle, a union member and democratic voter, kept his sense of humor. He said it "was where elephants go to die."

On at least one occasion I had stayed with him when I was a young teenager because my father had thrown me out of the house. I recalled vaguely that my uncle had called my father on the phone when I showed up at his house and told him, in my presence, that I was spending the rest of the weekend as his guest.

"The boy is staying with me this weekend," he said, harshly, expressing in his tone his disapproval to a friend, my father, on the phone. We ate TV dinners and drank Dixie beer for every meal that weekend, a new experience for a 14 year old.

"He was doing alright," I replied to her question, as I stretched out the phone cord so I could sit at the kitchen table.

"Did you get a chance to talk with him alone?" she asked.

"Yeah, thankfully no one else was there," I said. "He was in pretty good spirits and, in fact, he lectured me a little about when I was going to settle down."

"Sounds like a fun conversation," Caroline chided.

"Well, he has this grand theory about me, that everything I do is done because I need to rebel, for him that includes everything from not marrying to wearing red high-top tennis shoes." Caroline laughed.

"I'm 34 years old and it's a little distressing to me that a man who has known me my whole life could have such a singularly narrow view of my motivation. I guess that I have failed miserably at conveying the basis of my beliefs to him."

"I'm sure he meant no harm," Caroline offered in reply.

"I know that. He means the world to me. One of two or three people who took bullets for me when I was young and saved me from damnation," I said. "I guess I am a just a little sensitive about such things. Don't know why. It just bothers me that he sees everything I've ever done as simply unprincipled acts of rebellion."

"Well, Tusa, you do puzzle people. What's that saying of yours? 'I'm not like other birds of prey.' And classifying something as rebellion is probably just his way of trying to categorize things you have done so he can understand them. Every time someone challenges authority or dogma, or someone else's comfortable rituals, that happens," Caroline said. "But I'm surprised that someone classifying you as a rebel would really bother you," she concluded, insightfully. I paused for a moment and adjusted the phone against my ear.

"Well, 'bothers' is probably too strong. I guess it's an ego thing. I really don't like for someone to try to reduce all my beliefs to an unthinking cliché. I am uncomfortable with the implication that I take stands on issues just for the sake of rebelling. I hope my value system is a little more intricate than that. I don't know. It just feels marginalizing. I don't think anyone really knows me, other than you," I replied.

"Oh, I don't think rebellion characterizes your entire value system, but I've seen you do or say things on occasion just to provoke a response. In fact, I sometimes think that your role in my life is to keep me from getting too comfortable with my beliefs. You are the provoker, the protagonist, if you will, of my religious consciousness. I even mentioned that role to Loretta the other day," Caroline said.

"That role is not successful unless the other person is conscious and willing to think," I replied, a bit sarcastically. "Besides, you are referring principally to religious beliefs and my nonconformity," I said. I got out of the kitchen chair and walked over to the refrigerator to get something to drink.

"You may think it radical for me to say," Caroline stated, "but I think all rebellion, by definition, is linked in some fashion to religion."

I did not immediately respond to Caroline's statement, since I was trying to pour cranberry juice into a glass while holding the phone against my ear with my shoulder. Caroline continued.

"Christianity, at least Christ's actual teachings, are that we should identify with all of mankind. We should be our brother's keeper, so to speak, and not place ourselves above others. I have always thought that many acts of rebellion are not individualistic but, rather, are examples of individuals identifying with their brothers and sisters and, at least in their own minds, usually attempting to better everyone's condition. In other words, the desired result of the rebellious act may be hopelessly off course, but the intent of the act of rebellion is what is close to the premise of Christianity. I mean I know there can be exceptions, but I think there is a type of link," she said, ending awkwardly.

I had succeeded in pouring the glass of juice and returning the bottle to the refrigerator. I moved back toward my chair. "You're on a roll---continue." Caroline sighed a bit. "It's like the big bang theory you told me about, where the universe keeps expanding. Well, it's rebellion that is often the catalyst for the expansion of our humanity."

"You forget," I finally interrupted, "that lots of innocent people have been slaughtered or placed into servitude because of acts of rebellion, or during periods of rebellion. I'm not sure the rebel's actions are always altruistic," I said, uplifted by the conversation. "But since I have been in rebellion my whole life I hope you are right."

"I didn't say it was a perfect theory," she confided, in a lowered voice. "But realistically, a person has only a few choices. They can be religious, they can be apathetic, or they can be in rebellion against religion," she replied.

"I have bad news for you Caroline," I said.

"What's that?" she asked.

"Your theory is closer to Albert Camus' writings than that of Christianity," I replied.

"Obviously, Camus was inspired by Christ on these points," she said, in a very sensuous voice. I couldn't restrain my laughter.

FORTY-SEVEN

~

As I sat at the bar I heard James Booker's piano in the background on the jukebox. I used to see Booker on week nights at the Maple Leaf in the halcyon days when there were tables on what was now the dance floor. I had been fortunate enough to see a lot of good piano players over the years, from locals like Professor Longhair, Roosevelt Sykes, Dr. John and Huey "Piano" Smith, to so-called musical legends like Ray Charles, Champion Jack Dupree, and Jerry Lee Lewis. None of them compared to Booker.

"The Ivory Emperor," as Booker was sometimes called, was not only better on the piano, he was, to my ear, music personified. That is, he lived his melancholy life like a song in progress, authentically and tragically at the same time, in an unfamiliar dirge of a melody. There was little question he would end badly. He was pathologically temperamental; like the night he refused to play until some sorority types at a table stopped talking. He was playfully bipolar, like the night he stripped to his underwear and gave someone change to wash his clothes in the back Laundromat while he played. But mostly he was distant, a bit paranoid, playing the piano while looking away from the crowd, through the glass window into the street, as if he could only speak to us musically and needed to keep distance between himself and the rest of humanity, which he did not trust.

I listened intently as the jukebox played his rendition of 'Junco Partner,' and I thought of those nights watching him play. I thought of our attempts from the crowd to calm him, encourage him, calling out "It's O.K. James," to get him to keep playing.

I let go of the memory and looked at the crowd. I had come to the bar tonight to try and think about what was happening to me and why childhood questions now seemed so important. I had no answers and barely any questions. But I felt the malignancy of it knotting up inside of me, a physical manifestation of some growing psychic malady.

I thought hard about my brother's story concerning my attempt to go to art camp. It remained just a story as nothing about it seemed familiar. No single detail felt real to me. I had no sense that I had lived it. Where were such memories buried and why were those memories, or the harm associated with those memories, seeking to unearth themselves now? I still didn't know.

FORTY-EIGHT

~

I could not believe it when I thought about it. I had probably said it hundreds of times during sex. I never knew why I had whispered it. It had just seemed natural, as if I grew up with it. Now, suddenly, it was like I was realizing for the first time what I had actually been saying. It was like someone had written it on the blackboard of a class I was taking and I was strapped in a chair and forced, eyes wide open, Clockwork Orange like, to read it. I had to read it aloud repeatedly, over and over and over, from the chair. I had to read and absorb each word while seated. I had to study it alone and outside of the sex act.

I looked at the imaginary blackboard. The words mocked me. I saw myself saying to a woman repeatedly, "it's alright, it's only me." I saw myself saying it in a comforting tone. I saw myself saying it in a tone designed to reassure a woman on the verge of an orgasm. I saw myself saying it in a tone designed to reassure a woman whose body shuttered in the throes of an orgasm.

What did it mean? Why did I say it? Had it ever been said to me? It suddenly seemed inappropriate. It seemed to reflect a desire to assure my partner that it was alright to have sex with me because, after all, it was "only me." Was that simply a deeper insecurity, or did it forebode something more sinister?

My mind searched in the dark for any spark of recollection. Everything remained blank. I realized the possible connection to my youth; to assure me, as a child, of the improper; to be used by someone of authority; to molestation by someone close to me. I could not bring anything forward. I could not recall anything, just a sense of unease.

It was another piece of information to store, to periodically roll over in my mind and examine. The pieces were gathering up, corroding the iron bars, and slowly undermining me.

I had recalled when writing my list of childhood memories, that I had slept with the covers over my head at least until I was 11 or so, the time period when my first memories began. Every night I would lay down and fearfully pull the covers over my head exposing only my nose and mouth to the air outside the covers. As I thought of that memory, I tried to also recall the presumed fear associated with covering my head with the covers. It was a fear I couldn't bring forward. That fear must have been the reason for "hiding" under the covers. Was it just childishness, or did it portend something else? I could not discern anything further about the cause of the fear but, for a brief moment, I reached blindly for its contours. Its origin, however, was unknown to me.

I considered starting a list of ideas that were occurring to me, or of odd behaviors I was recalling as things were falling out of my grasp. I was still fighting, still on the husk of discovery, seeking to defend myself against the potential pain. But I was losing, the tide of my discontent was coming in and washing away my sand castle barriers.

FORTY-NINE

~

I had thought long and hard about Caroline's suggestion that I ask my brother to tell me more stories of my childhood. Something was still holding me back. I wondered if I had been an abuser of him? I recalled having read theories of abused children becoming abusers of siblings. The thought sickened me.

In thinking about it, I thought, perhaps for the first time in years, about the effect of my childhood, not on me, but on my brother. On some days those splintering thoughts nearly broke me. I found myself becoming emotional over his childhood, even though I could not recall it. By all accounts that I had heard, my parents were not as physically abusive to him as they were to me. If someone was to get a beating it was usually me.

But my brother, it seemed to me, from my current developing perspective, suffered through my childhood in a much different and less recognized fashion. He became the child ignored, the purposely quiet one. The one my mother would say, in contrast to me, "was no trouble at all." He was the child who lived in the obscurity of the battles between my father and me, or my mother and me. While he probably did not suffer the belittlement and ridicule, which I apparently did, he may have suffered from a neglect of attention. He suffered from a lack of substantive attention precisely because I was always noncompliant, claiming their tired attention.

In thinking about it, I did recall one instance, although I could not place it in time, when he and I got into a fight. More than likely, as the older brother, I simply beat him up. My father responded severely. Although I do not remember specifically what he did to me, I recalled that he told me if I ever put my hands on my brother again I would "regret it for the rest of my life." A threat of harm I knew well and took seriously. At that point the bond of brotherhood, through no fault of my brother, was broken. I ignored him more forcefully. It was something neither he or I ever understood or discussed, but it was part of my self-preservation, a forced line drawing by me in order to stay safe.

As a result of my thinking about our relationship, I decided I was not comfortable approaching my brother and asking that he tell me about my childhood. I would have to discuss it with him at some point, but I needed to start elsewhere. I knew that there were only two other primary sources of information about my childhood, my parents. I resolved that if I were going to broach the subject with anyone it would have to first be with my father.

I had mixed emotions about that resolution. I had no desire to retaliate, no desire to hurt him or my mother by raising issues regarding my treatment as a child. I'm sure I had caused them enough pain over my adult years by disassociating. I was caught in a quandary over whether raising the issue would be too painful for my father and my own personal need to know more about what happened. But I realized I had no choice. I was entangled and being pulled down by the emotions of it now. My father readily conceded that he had made some "mistakes" when I was young, but we had never talked substantively about those mistakes, or their effects on me or on him.

I had returned to New Orleans in 1977 after a two-year hiatus from the family, a prodigal son who had not fallen on his face, who had not failed as prophesized. During those two years I tended bar, made some money, lived with my girlfriend, and he and I spoke infrequently. Upon returning to town in 1977 to return to college again a slow tentative rapprochement began.

I was naturally apprehensive about devoting time to developing a relationship with my parents upon returning to town. I imposed my own guidelines in numerous conversations with my father that I'm certain were baffling to him. For example, I told my father that I would not refer to him as "dad" and would not allow him to call me "son." Indeed, anger would rise up in me anytime anyone, for any reason, called me "son." Those words, "dad" and "son," I told him firmly, had meant nothing when I was growing up and I would not now pretend they had some artificial meaning. I told him if a relationship was to build between us it would have to be on the basis of friendship. I would not be close to him simply because of biological ties. Although I was never sure he completely understood my motives, he silently consented to my prerequisites and in doing so, maybe for the first time, our roles began to change. He began to speak to me and not at me. My father turned out to be a better friend to me than a parent. Perhaps, like me, he better understood the dynamics of a friendship than the demands of unconditional love expected of a father-son relationship.

FIFTY

~

o that religion, the Christian religion especially, became dual. The religion of the strong taught renunciation and love and the religion of the weak taught down with the strong and let the poor be glorified. Since there are always more weak people, than strong, in the world, the second sort of Christianity has triumphed and will triumph,'" I read.

"Stop," she said. I lowered the book by D. H. Lawrence and looked at her. Caroline shook her head negatively. "I have serious trouble with this guy's logic," she said coarsely.

"Well," I interrupted, "in support of your confusion, I believe Lawrence was dying when he wrote *Apocalypse*, so his thought process may have been fractured. However, his point in this quotation is pretty simple. Sounds a lot like Nietzsche."

"Well, it's all one religion," she said. "I'm not following his claim of duality."

"Maybe we shouldn't have jumped ahead in the book," I replied. "My recollection is that Lawrence is talking about the difference between what Jesus taught and what the church has done with what he has taught."

"So he concedes Jesus lived," Caroline stated.

"Yes, I believe he concedes that Jesus was a prophet," I said, as I thumbed through the earlier pages of the book.

"See here, a bit earlier in the book he lays out the duality argument a bit more," I said handing the book to Caroline.

"All right," she said after scanning the page. "How is it, or why is it, in his opinion, that the church took the wrong path?"

"I don't recall his specifics on that point, except that he believes that church dogma is more rooted in the Book of Revelations than in Christ's actual teachings," I said. Caroline laughed, covering her mouth with her hand, reflecting a southern charm I had never noticed.

"That's crazy," she said. "The Book of Revelations has never made any sense to me. It is full of pagan references like the seven sons of the seven daughters and such nonsense. It's a screed against Nero, isn't it? How can he argue that church teachings are based on a book in the Bible that makes so little sense? What about the commandments? Or Christ's teachings in Matthew to love God and your fellow man? Those make up the foundation of Christianity?"

"Lawrence disagrees that the church principles are founded on the commandments, or on much of Christ's teachings, and I tend to agree with him. The Bible says nothing about a whole host of things that churches preach as dogma and that the congregation is supposed to believe," I said.

"Examples?" Caroline requested.

"In the Catholic Church, there is the doctrine of papal infallibility, which you won't find anywhere in Christ's teachings. It's a political doctrine that arose centuries after Christ died, in the 1800s. Many churches don't allow kids to attend their schools unless their parents donate to the church. You also won't find that in Christ's teachings," I said. "The Catholic Church doesn't allow women to be priests and requires that it's priests remain celibate. Where is that in the Bible, or in the commandments?" I asked rhetorically. "The list is really endless," I said.

"Well, I don't think of any of those things when I think of Christianity. It's not about a church, or a priest, or the rules of church membership. It's much more personal to me," Caroline replied. "And it starts with accepting the concept of grace and is grounded in the lessons of the Sermon on the Mount. Nevertheless, what about the link with the Book of Revelations?" she asked.

"I think Lawrence's point, if I understand it correctly, is that the Book of Revelations, written by John of Patmos while in prison, tries to raise up for exultation the meek and the poor and put down the rich and successful. I think he argues that the churches have followed that approach to Christianity, marketing themselves, and pandering to the downtrodden. In a sense, the churches have advertised themselves as the great equalizer for the downtrodden, since the meek even have a better chance of getting into heaven than the rich man has of passing through the eye of a needle, or some such thing," I said. Caroline laughed again.

"That's is silliness," she said, as I turned a few pages in the book. "I realize some people believe that stuff, but it is so foreign to my notion of Christianity. Being a Christian has nothing to do with one's bank account and everything to do with how you treat others," she replied.

I silently read another section of the book as Caroline looked on. "Lawrence says that there are two types of Christianity," I summarized. "One is focused on the command to love by Jesus and the other is focused on the apocalypse and glorifying the meek," I said.

Caroline pursed her lips contemplating what I had said.

FIFTY-ONE

~

My brother Nicholas rang the door bell to my house. I could see him through the front window and got up to open the door. He had asked me earlier in the week if he could borrow my chain saw. The chain saw was in my back shed, so, after briefly exchanging perfunctory greetings, we walked through the hall of the house toward the backdoor.

The shed was about 20 yards from the house's back door. I had not ventured out into it in a few months. I was not even sure where the chain saw was, since I had not used it in a while.

"It may need oil," I said to him, as we walked.

"OK. I'll clean it up after I use it. Just need it for the weekend," he replied.

Once the shed door was open and the overhead light was on, I looked around the clutter for the orange frame of the saw. Nicholas was looking over my shoulder and he pointed. "Over there," he said.

I stepped over some lumber and balanced on my right foot while I leaned toward a table to reach for the chain saw. I stumbled and bumped hard into the table with my torso as I was reaching. A hammer fell from the table and landed on the top of my right foot. I clenched my teeth and tightened my face muscles. I picked my foot up for a moment and hopped on the good foot once or twice. I did not make a sound. I then grabbed the handle of the chain saw and picked it up. I turned to face the door and my brother, with the chain saw in my hand.

"Shit, that must have hurt," Nicholas said.

"Yeah, it did," I replied.

I moved out of the shed and handed the chain saw to Nicholas. As we walked down the driveway, I could feel the top of my foot throbbing. I was limping.

"You still don't make any noise when you get hurt," Nicholas said, in a matter-of-fact tone. "Boy, does that bring back memories," he stated. I didn't understand what he was talking about. I thought for a moment and realized that, as best I could recall, he was right. I rarely said "ouch" or anything of the sort when I nicked myself, or bumped into something, around the house or elsewhere.

"I wonder why that is?" I asked aloud, more to myself than to Nicholas.

"More childhood baggage," Nicholas said directly, shifting the chain saw to his other hand so he could lift it up into the back of his pick-up truck.

"What do you mean?" I asked, as we stopped by the truck and he set the chain saw down in the bed of the truck.

"Well, it's just a guess, but I recall when you were 9 or 10 you told me in our bedroom that you were never going to cry again when dad hit you. You said *no matter what* you would no longer cry when he hit you. And after that you never cried when he hit you, or when you hurt yourself," Nicholas said, looking away, perhaps feeling the weight of the story's history. "No matter how bad the beating you never made a sound," he said.

I could not recall any such discussion with my brother. I also could not recall making such a promise to myself, though it sounded like something I might say.

Nicholas started to make his way to the driver side door of the truck. As he got into the truck, I stepped clear of it so he could back out. I felt the throbbing of my foot. He reached for the ignition key, he shook his head slightly and turned and looked at me. "It just pissed the old man off more." He turned the ignition key and when the engine started, reached out with his left hand and closed the truck door.

I waved at him as he slowly backed out of the driveway. As he pulled away from the house Caroline drove up. She got out of her car with a book in her hand and full of energy, as I limped forward to hug her.

"What happened to you?" she asked.

"Nothing. I'm just getting old," I replied, as we entered my house.

FIFTY-TWO

~

We sat quietly reading on opposite ends of the sofa. In the background on the stereo, a cassette of R. Carlos Nakai, the native American flute player, and Peter Kater, the pianist, played. Caroline often put their music on as "background music" when she read. Although I could not articulate why, I recognized a spiritual, a healing, aspect to the music.

Coincidentally, I was trying to finish a novel entitled, *House Made of Dawn*, by N. Scott Momaday. The Native American flute was an appropriate background for reading about Abel and the Eagle Watchers Society. Caroline was reading Faulkner's *A Fable*. We had been sitting and reading for at least an hour.

When the cassette reached the end of side two I got up and put in another of the Nakai/Kater tapes she had brought to the house. I asked Caroline if she wanted something to drink. She said she did and, as she set her book down on the coffee table, got up from the sofa and followed me into the kitchen.

I poured us both a glass of iced tea. We stood in the kitchen in the intimate silence of two who knew each other well without the complications of being lovers. It was a connection beyond words that was more involved than either of us would ever completely understand. I normally moved at a hundred miles an hour in my life, racing, running. Perhaps afraid to slow down and be found out. The unspoken and unacknowledged fear so common of being found shallow. But with Caroline time slowed down for me and I often did as well, without fear.

"I appreciate you allowing me to just come by and read," Caroline finally said, breaking the silence. Caroline moved to the kitchen table and pulled out a chair and sat down.

"I don't know if you know what our friendship means to me," she said, more seriously, as I moved to sit with her at the table. "I mean, I don't believe I have ever expressed it properly to you," she said, directly, holding her glass of tea with both hands in front of her. I looked at her and noticed that her pupils had increased in size. Long ago Rebekah had told me that a person's pupil size increases when they are looking at a kindred spirit, at someone they love. I had laughed at the time in response.

I hesitated, a male stumble, and replied that I guess I had never said much about the importance of the friendship either.

"You," Caroline said softly, but then stopped. Her eyes began to fill with tears and I saw her roll her lips inward to stop them from quivering. I reached out one of my hands and put it on the table palm up. She removed one of her hands from the glass and placed it in mine.

"You are probably the best thing that could happen to my faith," she finally said, her voice quivering. "You constantly force me to think about my life, about my beliefs, about who I am. You don't realize how rare such an approach is to life," she said.

"You force me to do the same thing," I then said, in an equally unsteady tone, with emotion powering into me. "There are very few people left who are willing to reflect on their lives," I said more quietly, while gently rubbing my thumb on the top of her hand.

"But there are times when you need to let it go," she said, teacher to pupil. "There are times when you will need to simply believe and not analyze something further. Because," she said, clearing her throat of concern, "faith, whether in God or any other relationship, is based on emotion, not on your intellect."

I listened and did not respond. There were times for argument and there were times for me to simply listen to Caroline, or for her to listen to me. I was still learning the difference, making missteps often, but I got it right this time.

"It seems to me that something is going on with you right now that you are trying to keep locked up. There is the appearance of emotion, strong emotion, for the first time since I have known you, forcing you to leave the island of your intellect. Perhaps it's related to family issues, but, perhaps, it's the result of something larger going on inside you," she said. She stopped and leaned forward slightly. I still did not speak, but I kept my eyes on her face. Tears welled in her eyes again and fell down her cheeks. "It may be part of the grieving process, steps in the Kubler-Ross 5 stages of grief, over your childhood," she said. She then put her other hand on top of my hand on the table. I felt tears also forming in my eyes, moved again by the thought of her unconditional love. She looked down at my hand.

"Just let it happen," she said, and squeezed my hand affectionately with both of hers.

"I'm trying," I stammered.

FIFTY-THREE

~

He taught me carpentry, how to use a skil-saw, a chop saw and a table saw. He taught me how to pop a chalk line, to use a plumb bob, how to use a level and chisel. I watched and learned from him how to assemble and perform plumbing as needed. He tried to teach me about electricity, but I had a mental block and could never remember the basics, even the ground versus live wires. Just a mental block. He took apart car engines, while instructing his distracted son, and easily tuned them. He showed me how to work on an old slant six engine in my first car, a 1964 Dodge Dart.

And I was realizing that his own demons, the ones he would not confront, pushed him to instill in me a numbing survival instinct. He had been through a theology of brutality as a child and as a combat Marine in Korea. He wanted his first-born son, his namesake, to be tougher, to be able to survive whatever insolence and despair society heaped on him. But the problem, the problem he never solved in his own life, was that the cultivation of a survival instinct meant dulling all your emotions and waiting, waiting in anticipation of the next inevitable hammer blow to fall. At the same time, or maybe as a result, he thought that life was something you had to conquer, an unending Darwinian fight. I'm certain he felt he was giving me the tools to do so, to survive in such an adversarial world, but his error was, in part, that these were tools molded in the fires of his experiences, not mine. But by becoming abusive to me, succumbing to his father's brutal legacy, he remained a captive, and destroyed his only chance to be free.

Whenever I figured out a way to fix something that was broken, to, against all logic, make it work again, I think of those many lessons he taught me. My father was a jack of all trades and a master of many. He understood, implicitly, and with little formal education, engines, electricity, and if he took something apart to learn about it, he owned it thereafter, except for the screw or two that was always left over.

He gave my brother and me countless humorous sayings that covered the waterfront of human experience. If we were caught loafing instead of working, he would chastise us by saying: "You have your thumb up your ass and your mind in Arkansas." A saying I still don't understand. If he met someone who he thought was stupid, he said: "That guy is so dumb he couldn't pour piss out of a boot if the directions to do so were written on the heel."

He had seen the face of death up close as a soldier too many times. Yet he could be silly, the adolescent he was never allowed to be, with a great heartfelt laugh, especially away from my mother. On fishing trips with his childhood friend Angelo it was a comedy routine, one playing off the other. And he was tough, never showing the bluebird in his heart, as Bukowski wrote. Marine Corp tough. Maybe he had to be. He was the smallest of his brothers, the smallest of Marines having to get a waiver because of his size, and, according to my uncle, could take a hell of a punch and then stand and deliver one with a force twice his size. And underneath it all, under that snarling tough guy veneer, beneath the fist fights when younger, and the man who told his kids that you only get sick if you let yourself, was a man who confided to me once, only once, that he was afraid of the dark.

I finally raised the issue of my childhood with my father. I really had no choice as it was becoming obvious to my father that something was bothering me and it was disrupting my life. I had begun to avoid him and my mother again. I couldn't explain why. But I was still uncomfortable with asking questions, as if by doing so I would finally get my wings with answers, only to experience Icarus' fate and fly too close to the sun.

FIFTY-FOUR

~

When I asked him directly, my father denied that anything had occurred to me when I was young. He laughed awkwardly when I asked him if I had ever been molested. I asked if I had ever even made such a claim. He said "no," abruptly, definitively. I asked if he could think of anything that occurred when I was young related to sexual molestation. He moved uncomfortably in his chair from the question and advised that he could think of nothing that would even remotely suggest that I might have been molested.

He advised me that what occurred, "very simply," he said, without a pause, "was that at five or six years of age you decided that you would not listen to your parents anymore and that you didn't want to have anything to do with us." That, he said, was the cause of most of the confrontations between myself and my parents.

"It wasn't me. It was you. You were the problem," he said emphatically, with his hands folded in his lap, seated in his favorite lounge chair. I listened patiently as he spoke to me in a rehearsed voice of patriarchal disapproval, the voice of a Marine staff sergeant, that I knew well and that brooked no dissent, and demanded obedience.

"One more thing. I'm not going to feel guilty about anything I've done in the past," he said, launching his counter offensive. The voice that confronted me growing up with such authority, that had likely cowered me as a child, had no effect on me, no hold on the child that he had raised to become a man.

I told him my purpose was not to make him feel guilty, but that I was going to keep asking questions. He told me that I should do whatever I felt I needed to do and he would be supportive. He was being evasive. The past was something in his own life which he always refused to examine. It had to be disquieting that his son was going to do to him what he had feared doing with his father.

I had lived for too long within the closed walls of my family when I was younger. Having left those confines and having spent years examining those walls, from the inside and from the outside, and grown too big to return, I knew all too well how my family dynamics worked. My father was the product of a very manipulative father. Indeed, by all accounts his father was a beast, locking his children under the house, beating them with chains, throwing them into china cabinets and threatening to kill them. My father retained some of his father's manipulative characteristics, despite his best efforts. He had been rejected too often as a child by his father and siblings, spent a lifetime seeking his father's approval, and as an adult aggressively sought to eliminate the chance of any future rejections by those closest to him. I wondered if this was a trait, a genetic descent with modification, that he unknowingly passed on to me, the fear of rejection, and was part of my ongoing internal battle. He also had numerous things in his life that he had chosen not to examine. "I'm too old to bring that up now," he would say to me at various points in his life. I was taking a different path. Ironically, the childhood physical abuse that likely forced me to live in my head, was a far safer place from which to examine the rocks and psychological mortar that made up my own walls.

Within two weeks of my conversation with my father, as if it was always waiting for me, I had spoken with several childhood friends and relatives and learned that two neighborhood friends had been molested when we were children. I also learned that one of my father's friends, a Catholic priest, was a pedophile. The priest, according to my brother, occasionally played golf with my father on weekends and was periodically at our house. There was a lawsuit pending against the priest by former students who alleged molestation. The priest had, for a while, been the associate pastor at the Catholic grammar school I attended before being sent to another. I had no personal recollection of the priest although his name sounded vaguely familiar. I obtained copies of the case pleadings from a friend who, coincidentally, represented the Catholic archdiocese in the litigation by the former students against the priest. Nothing seemed to fit, as the children the priest was accused of molesting were young girls from a school I did not attend.

I also learned from my aunt that one of my father's brothers, who died young, had been molested as an adolescent. The brother became bisexual. A secret not discussed at all in the family.

I learned many other things during those discussions, family secrets if you will, some of which did not seem relevant at the time. My father, for example, had been sent to the seminary while in the seventh grade. He apparently quit shortly thereafter. He took a bus home from Lafayette and then walked home from the bus station in New Orleans. His father was upset with him for having quit the seminary, told him he had embarrassed the family and threatened to kill him. My father had steadfastly refused to discuss his time in the seminary, or what happened while he was there, with anyone, though he slipped once and told me it was there that he first met a gay priest. My Sicilian grandfather, my father's father, had also shot and killed a black man in the 1920's for merely walking into the whites only side of the barroom, the Rendon Inn, he owned.

It was childhood friends, my brother, my aunt, my uncle, a cousin, and the parents of a childhood friend who filled in the details of my childhood. I learned that my father felt my 20 year old mother was incapable of dealing with a newborn child so he would drop me off, as a baby, with the nuns at the Catholic convent next door to my parents' first home before going to work in the morning. For how many months, or years this occurred, no-one could recall. My father, apparently, also had the habit, when I was young and misbehaved, of threatening to drop me off at an orphanage.

I learned that my father was often gone working long hours when my brother and I were very young. I was told that I would receive "whippings" between two to four times a month. The "whippings" were apparently more frequent during the summer break from school when there was more time for conflict. My brother, who I finally spoke to, confided that I would sometimes volunteer that I did something even when I knew that he had done the act in question. He said that when he asked I would shrug my shoulders and say I was going to get hit anyway. Somewhere in the processing of all this information, I realized that I often used sayings, inculcated childhood things, the genesis of which had been unknown to me, like "I'd rather take a beating," in describing uncomfortable situations confronting me as an adult.

These things sat with me, cathartic, in the open air, but I did not know what to do with the information. I couldn't find all the pieces of my lost memory, part of the story of who I had become, but still the process mattered. In fact, despite these efforts, I would never learn exactly what happened to me as a child.

There was still no equilibrium established between my emotions and intellect from these discoveries. At least not yet. That would have to wait for unexpected events.

FIFTY-FIVE

~

You are going to have to run that theory by me again," she said, with a quizzical look on her face, as we sat in the early evening at a coffee shop on Julia street. Loretta sat next to her but reflected no emotion in response. While Caroline was animated as she thought about the concept, Loretta was a portrait of purposeful apathy. She stared at an empty package of sugar which she was rolling between the thumbs and forefingers of her hands.

"Where do you think up these theories anyway?" Caroline said, with a school girl grin and looking from me to Loretta for support. I ignored her question and continued with my explanation.

"The basic idea is that all of us, men anyway, to varying degrees, seek avenues for asserting our power, or displaying that we have some social power," I said. "Because power is an evolutionary attraction. Ask any woman." Caroline frowned at the premise. "Anyway, sexual prowess is simply a manner of expressing social power. My theory is that the less social power a man has in vehicles like business, education, etc., the more likely it is that his attempts at sexual prowess will be his expression of social power. Likewise, the more social power a man has through business, the less likely sexual prowess will be used by him as his sole expression of social power," I said, as if reciting something I had read.

"So what you are saying is the less successful someone is in business the more likely he is to be good in bed?" Caroline asked, shaking her head in humor at the thought.

"Actually, it is more like the fewer avenues available to a man to succeed at business and at his chosen profession, the more likely he is to try to be good in bed, or at least to use sex as his attempt to convey his power," I replied.

"So have you gotten better or worse since you became a partner in the law firm?" Caroline asked, and then laughing clapped her hands lightly in front of her.

"I have gotten worse since I started practicing law," I replied, in my best analytical tone. Caroline laughed again, as I smiled at her.

"How does your theory apply to women?" Loretta suddenly asked, in a more serious tone. She continued, however, to look only at the rolled sugar package between her fingers. I paused. I had not expected the question.

"I guess as women become more and more involved in the working world, suffer the same stressors, and attempt to achieve the same standards of success in business and other areas as males, they will suffer the same problems. Maybe evolve in the same direction," I said. Caroline turned to face Loretta.

"You're not buying this silliness, are you?" Caroline asked incredulously.

"It's an interesting idea," Loretta said, in an almost mono-tone voice. "I think Norman Mailer wrote something similar," she concluded.

"I thought it was Eldridge Cleaver," I said.

"I think it was Mailer," she replied. "What have you read of Eldridge Cleaver?"

"*Soul on Ice.* I'm not aware that he wrote anything else," I said. Loretta then turned to Caroline without a further glance at me.

"Have you read that book?" she asked. Caroline indicated that she had not. I could sense that Loretta was moving to exclude me from the conversation. At the same time, I had the feeling that Loretta was surprised I had read Eldridge Cleaver. I recalled that Cleaver had remarkable insight about the correlation between the white man's oppression of blacks and the white man's mistreatment of white women. Loretta stopped talking.

A few minutes later I excused myself so that I could stop for a drink and then return home. It was early and I wanted to get some sleep. I was trying to bring some normalcy back into my life. Maybe drink a bit less, think a bit more about what I had learned concerning my childhood and regain my footing.

FIFTY-SIX

~

One of Caroline's remarks about the cause of my lack of religious belief kept coming back to me and seemed to dovetail with my struggles over my childhood experiences. I kept recalling her statement about the possible correlation between not being able to believe in God and childhood issues with my father. The idea, strangely enough, was slowly starting to make sense to me. I was by no means ready to embrace it wholeheartedly, but felt there was more to the correlation, some deeper psychological link, than I had previously admitted.

I reached over and grabbed a rock glass on the night stand which had a swallow of Kendall Jackson Cabernet left in it. I sat up in bed and turned and looked at Tammy, a woman I had met out the night before when I stopped for a drink after meeting Caroline and Loretta at the coffee shop. Tammy was laying next to me with the pillow pulled under her head and chest. She had a yellow and black butterfly, Swallowtail, tattooed on the back of her right shoulder. I drank the remainder of the warm wine, grimaced as it went down, and then held the glass with both hands in my lap.

It seemed to me that the critical issue in Caroline's theory, was the ability to have faith in someone or something. Perhaps the net effect of my childhood was to destroy in me that part which could believe instead of knowing. The idea was that my childhood somehow resulted in me always demanding proof, or at least being fearful of faith. That might also explain the intellectual fortress I had built.

The idea was intriguing but bothersome. To the extent that my atheism was a result, even indirectly, of my childhood abuses, it meant, at the least, Caroline's notion of a relative free will. I was not ready to accept such an idea, even if I felt that absolute free will was untenable in reality. I suspect part of the reason for my hesitancy was my own philosophical desire, or was it inculcated by my father, to be completely responsible for myself and my actions. I often saw complete responsibility for self as the basis of my moral code. Religion and restricted free will, or no free will, undermined personal responsibility.

I must have drifted off a bit in my semi seated position. When I woke, Tammy was seated facing me with her legs folded underneath her. She leaned forward and kissed me on the lips. She stared at me, smiled easily and waited for some recognition from me. I stared back and, the victory having been achieved, smiled less easily, wondering what might be expected of me now. She then sat back and told me that I had been mumbling something about having no home to go to and she did not know whether to wake me.

I thought and recalled that in the dream I appeared at my parent's house looking for a place to stay for the night, but was sent away by my father. "You don't live here," he said, closing the door on me. In the dream, I wandered away looking for a place to sleep. I recognized this as a variation of an increasingly recurrent dream of mine in which I was homeless and briefly wondered what Jungian symbols were growing out of this persistent dream. I was surprised to hear her say I was speaking out loud while sleeping.

"I really don't recall my childhood in a first person sense," I confided, somewhat nonchalantly, and involuntary, as I looked away from her, unable to meet her gaze. She pulled her long hair back behind her head and twirled it five or six times before letting it fall.

"That could reflect an abused childhood---or just a bad memory," she said to me, lowering her hands and then laying them against her black pubic hair.

I heard her remark, but did not absorb it immediately. I had only met this woman the night before, still had my guard up, and paused as I considered whether to discuss any aspect of my life in detail.

"You should read Alice Miller's book *The Drama of a Gifted Child*," she offered. "You might get some insight from it."

"I was hardly a 'gifted' child," I replied too abruptly, defensively, emphasizing the word 'gifted'. I then found myself struggling to gain control of the conversation as Tammy kept instructing me on things I should consider about my childhood.

"I survived my childhood," I finally said. "We are all prisoners of our parents' successes and fuck-ups. I am aware of some of the effects of my childhood and I try to deal with these as best I can. I am not convinced, however, that there is a childhood experience lurking behind my every action."

"You seem pretty hostile about it, which suggests you have not dealt with it," she said firmly, undeterred, as she started getting off the bed. I thought to myself that everyone these days seemed to be a self-proclaimed therapist.

"Is it alright if I take a shower? I have to be at work in an hour," she then asked. I stared at her body. She had a hard, lean and attractive body.

"Sure," I replied in a calm tone, resuming my role. When she got to the bedroom door she leaned into the door frame and turned back toward me.

"You can join me if you like. We have time." I got out of bed, walked over to her, slow and seductive, intimating that, perhaps, I wasn't interested, and, as she stood in the door way, kissed her like a soldier boarding a ship for war. She slowly kissed my neck and then began to work her way down my chest to my waist. I recalled the lyrics to a Michael Franks song that went something like "your secret's safe with me."

FIFTY-SEVEN

~

I was still searching for anchors of understanding from my intellect, so I began reading more philosophy. I was really surprised by what I had discovered. I was hopeful of finding Caroline at Café Brasil, a coffee shop, which she told me she had recently taken to stopping by on Sunday mornings before going to church. As I walked into the coffee shop, I quickly located her sitting alone at a table. She was reading a book. As I got closer, I realized it was the Bible. It struck me, momentarily, that I might be intruding on her private time. However, before I could veer off my course to her table, she saw me, smiled and waved me to come over. As I approached her table she stood up and hugged me. I noticed that there was a thin cloth bookmark on a page in the Bible. As we sat, Caroline adjusted the bookmark and closed the Bible.

"Don't tell me you have decided to come to church with me today?" she asked excitedly, but expecting disappointment.

"I thought you went earlier in the morning," I replied.

"No, the service is in a half-hour," she answered.

Caroline had always indicated that she had two immediate wishes about our friendship. The dichotomy between the two wishes reflected her uniqueness. Her first wish, which she often stated, was that I go with her to church on a Sunday. She did not go to one church. Rather, she would go to several over a month's time and then return to the ones she liked for a few months. Sometimes it was the priest or deacon which attracted her back, other times it was the architecture of the church, and still on other occasions it was a parishioner she had met. I recall that she would frequently say that she was meeting an elderly neighbor, or a recent acquaintance, at mass at a certain church.

The other wish she had for me she had only expressed once and, unlike the church request, in doing so she had elicited a promise from me. Odd as it may have seemed to her churchgoing friends, Caroline enjoyed her experiences with psychedelic mushrooms as a teenager. She told me one night how, the three or four times that she had done mushrooms, she had felt extraordinarily spiritual and peaceful. She explained that each time she had done the mushrooms with grape Kool-aid to cut the taste of the mushroom juice. I promised her that at some point, although I had never taken any drugs other than alcohol, I would drink some grape-Kool-aid-mushroom tea with her.

People were generally surprised that, long hair and all, I had never experimented with drugs, not even marijuana. But there was a simple explanation. When we were adolescents my father gave my brother and me one of his commandments.

"I don't care if you drink alcohol. I do it. But if you are ever caught with drugs there are only two things that can happen. You will either rot in jail if arrested, cause I'm not getting you out. Or if I catch you I will kill you." We both took the threat to heart.

"Actually, I was thinking about you because I ran across something that I thought we might think about."

"What is it?" she asked.

"Well, you remember the existentialist writer from France, Jean-Paul Sartre?" I asked.

"Only that you have mentioned him and, I think, that you indicated he was an atheist," she replied.

"Right. Well, Sartre . . ." At that point I leaned back in the chair and pulled out of my pocket a crumpled piece of loose leaf paper. I unfolded it on the table.

"Okay," I said, "Sartre wrote this:

What is meant here by saying that existence precedes essence? It means that first of all, man exists, turns up, appears on the scene, and only afterwards defines himself. If man, as the existentialist conceives him, is indefinable, it is because at first he is nothing. Only afterward will he be something, and he himself will have made what he will be. Thus, there is no human nature, since there is no God to conceive it. Not only is man what he conceives himself to be, but he is also only what he wills himself to be after this thrust toward existence.

"Now, here's the thing that I have found," I said. "Aquinas, the Catholic saint, wrote: ". . . in every created thing essence is distinct from existence and is compared to the latter as potentiality is to act."

I lifted my eyes from the paper on the table and looked at Caroline. "It's interesting to me that Sartre and Aquinas seem to both agree, in slightly different language, that existence precedes essence," I said. Caroline asked me to read the Aquinas' quotation again. She stated that she was not convinced that Aquinas meant the same thing as Sartre, but she conceded that he could be read as rejecting the notion of human nature.

"But Aquinas was as much a philosopher as theologian, wasn't he?" she asked.

"He was certainly a fan of Aristotle and used Aristotelian logic in the *Metaphysics*," I replied.

Caroline did not respond readily to a couple of points I made concerning the nature of responsibility if existence precedes essence. She was polite, but seemed disinterested. I realized that she may have been right about the Aquinas quote. For the first time in our relationship I also realized that I had interrupted something which was more important to Caroline than our friendship. She had been reading her Bible before going to church. I had barged in on this private time.

Although she told me not to worry about it, I apologized awkwardly for my intrusion. She seemed to blush a bit at the fact that I had realized the importance of this private time to her and that she had not succeeded at concealing it. I left her at the table alone and told her we would talk soon.

FIFTY-EIGHT

~

G ood news," I said, as I walked into Johnson's office. He looked up from his desk, clearly disinterested, as I approached. We had still not reconciled after the confrontation in the partnership meeting, but an uneasy truce, brokered by Singleton, existed.

"I think I've got the attorney representing the plaintiff in the *Cramer* case willing to accept a nominal settlement amount and dismiss the case."

"The *Cramer* case? Which case is that?" he asked. Christ, we had just talked about the case two days previously. Johnson was getting senile at forty-seven years old.

"The *Cramer* case is the death case where the decedent's widow alleged he died as a result of exposure to chemicals while on the job. We represent one of the chemical manufacturers, Vel-Tech," I said.

"Well, that case just came in a month or two ago," Johnson replied, leaning back easily in his chair.

"Right," I said, "but the guy is having trouble finding an expert witness so I thought it might be a good time to feel him out on a cheap settlement, and he seemed receptive."

"You can't settle that case, you have no authority and it's too early."

"Well, let's just check with the client. It's certainly cheaper for the client this way," I said. Johnson was silent for a moment. He placed both of his hands on his desk.

"You don't seem to understand that we can legitimately work that file over the next five or six months and make $40,000 or $50,000 in fees before its dismissal. . . ," he replied.

"---But, we have an obligation to the client to advise him that this matter can be settled right now," I interrupted. "If he pays a settlement of $2,500.00, he avoids paying all those fees. If he doesn't want to settle, that is his choice, not ours," I urged.

"Sit down! Now!" Johnson stated emphatically, more like yelling, as he rose from his chair in bluster; the truce was ending. "You are going to call the plaintiff's attorney and tell him there can be no settlement at this time. Then, I want you to transfer this file to Danny and let him work it up properly."

"I will not call opposing counsel and lie to him," I said, raising my voice. "We have an ethical obligation --"

"Shut up and listen to me!" he screamed, pointing his finger at me. "Don't you fucking lecture me on ethics! I'm sick of it!" he continued, losing his temper as he was prone to do, a deep insecurity with me that I had never understood. I got up from the chair and started to walk out of his office.

"Where are you going?" he yelled. "I'm talking to you -- you'll be fired for this!" he screamed.

"Go fuck yourself," I replied.

I walked past the secretaries' desks. They stared at me as if I was a leper who might infect them if I got too close. I heard Johnson slam his door and thought to myself about what a mediocre human being I had always considered him to be. He was a terrible phony, one that Holden Caulfield would have recognized at a glance. I couldn't believe I had put up with him for this long.

I walked into my office, sat down at my desk, and, without much forethought, wrote a note to one of the other senior partners, Singleton.

Effective the end of the month, I resign. Please see me if you have any questions.

I retrieved my coat and briefcase and walked to Singleton's office. I could hear him talking to Johnson in Johnson's office, trying to calm him down, with the door closed. I set my note on Singleton's desk. I had a meeting to go to outside the office and now was as good a time as any to leave.

FIFTY-NINE

~

I momentarily wondered if I had been too rash in resign-
ing. I knew that it was the only thing to do. I was tired of
the compromises, tired of who I was becoming, but I was
still uneasy with the decision. There seemed to be too many
things going on with me, too many battles, internal and external, which I was fighting at the same time. Maybe, with my
job resignation, I had simply chosen one thing that I could
cut free and could win. I had made no contingency plans as to
what I would do if I quit working for the firm. I really didn't
know whether to try to set up my own office, seek work with
another firm, or look for work outside of the legal profession.
I knew that the firm would systematically set out in the next
few weeks to try to cut off my contact with any clients. I felt
certain some clients would follow me if I continued practicing
law elsewhere, but whether it would be enough to pay bills and
make money was unclear. Unfortunately, the longer I waited,
the more difficult it would be for me to take clients wherever I
went. I needed to make a decision on my future soon.

As I contemplated what life might be like without a steady
income, I thought back to my days of poverty when I was in
college and in law school. In law school, I recalled living on
$300.00 per month. On that kind of income, I lived with a
roommate in the closed in garage of the bottom half of a stucco
double near the bus station, about a block from where the I-10
crossed over Florida Avenue in Baton Rouge. It was an area

that my more affluent white classmates politely described as a
"black neighborhood."

We had no air conditioning. We had no phone. For heat, we
had a very old space heater which made pinging noises while
operating and which we were both too frightened of to leave
on while we slept. Before going to bed in the wintertime, we
turned the heater off and slept with as many blankets as we
owned, or could borrow, on top of us. Generally, on very cold
nights, I slept in sweat pants.

Those were the days of checking the prices of every item at
the grocery store before deciding what to buy. Those were the
days of buying, exclusively, the grocery store's personal brand
of canned peas, carrots, string beans and potatoes, usually at
three or four cans for $1.00. Those store brand cans often had
rust on them and it was always wise to check to see if they were
swollen.

It was a time in my life when, if asked over for dinner by
someone, I went even if I was not particularly fond of them.
I learned to make a lot of Cole slaw using a 50 cent head of
cabbage and cheap mayonnaise. Those were also the days when
I went to the $1.99 all-the-salad-you-could-eat lunch specials
at the Pizza Hut. I would go from 11:00 a.m. to 2:00 p.m. on
the weekends and order the salad and a glass of water. The
waitresses would hate to see me show up.

Those were also the days of spending forty-five minutes at
the grocery store mulling over the best $2.00 bottle of wine to
buy.

And mice? Mice weren't too bad, unless they happened to
die in a wall in the house.

Poverty to me, whether in our house in the "black neighborhood" in Baton Rouge, or the small house trailer next to the
scrap metal yard in Lafayette that I lived in with a girlfriend
while in college, was never too bad, except for one thing. I

adapted to the sparse meals, to the lack of air conditioning, to the lack of heat, to the lack of a phone and the lack of spending money. It actually made life more simple.

The one thing about poverty to which I could not adapt was the fleas. No matter where I lived when I was very poor, there were fleas. What I remember most and liked least about having no money were the fleas.

SIXTY

~

I was leaning awkwardly into my car, a Renault Alliance, trying to remove a cassette tape that was stuck in the car's cassette player. I had pulled the car up next to the back porch and had all the car doors open. The cassette was not coming out. Caroline stood patiently on my porch watching me. She had come over to my house prior to heading out of town to Austin to visit her parents. She was contemplating accepting a job out of town in North Louisiana and said she wanted to see me before she left town. We had spoken about my resignation from the law firm, which she supported. I was going to head out of town as well for the weekend to try to decide what I should do next. She had been unusually clingy, hanging on to me, that morning when I opened the door for her to come inside. Oblivious to the needs of others, as I often was, I didn't know if she was trying to be supportive, or just needed a few hugs.

"Tusa, there was always something in the way. Every time I tried to tell you," she said, pacing back and forth, arms folded, in apparent contemplation, on the porch.

"What are you talking about?" I grunted, without looking at her, trying to get a pair of needle nose pliers to grip the cassette so I could pull it out.

"Tusa...the thing is, that you should know, is...I love you." I thought for a moment. Did I hear that right?

"What does that mean, Caroline? You mean you love me like a brother?" I asked automatically, without thinking. As soon as I said it I felt it sounded wrong.

"I'm in love with you," she said, strong, unafraid. I heard the words. Had anyone ever said that to me before and really meant it? Something forced me to get out of the car and stand up. She stood above me on the porch with a wide accepting smile on her face, waiting, slightly uncomfortable in her posture, but unburdened, looking at me. What should I say? I walked over to her, stepped up on the porch, and instinctively hugged her. She hugged me back, gently and put her hand at the base of my head. She then put her head on my shoulder. She tilted her head back to look right at me in expectation of a kiss. I kissed her briefly.

I grabbed her hand and walked her into the back yard. I felt the need to move. What should I say? My emotions were silent. Why couldn't I feel anything in response?

"I am not sure I am capable of love," I blurted out. Caroline remained calm. It was like she knew what to expect from me, my struggle with acceptance and with intimacy, and had anticipated my answer.

"I...If we were together...I ...I would get a lot out of that because of you, because of who you are," I heard myself say, faltering and unsure. My voice sounded hollow, echoed, and insincere. "But you would get the short end of the stick. I mean I'm no good at relationships, you've seen that. And cause I don't have anything to offer you."

"That's for me to decide. There's more to you than you realize," she replied, sincerely, without a trace of doubt. She squeezed my hand. I needed time to think. I felt unprepared.

"Kiss me again," she said less innocently. I leaned in and kissed her.

"Give me some time. I need to think about this," I said, unhappy with my intellectual response. I pulled her to me and hung on.

"Whatever you decide I just thought it was time that I tell you," she said, and then she nestled her head under my chin, childlike, but sensual. I am not sure I ever felt so empty.

After holding me tightly for awhile longer she kissed me again and then walked to her car to leave. Once in her car she waved at me and drove off. I returned to my attempt to get the cassette out of the cassette player so I could listen to some music when I left town early in the morning.

SIXTY-ONE

~

It was October 25, 1984," the announcer said on the NPR station on my car radio. I was on the road headed out of town for a few days to think about my future plans with work and now, in light of Caroline's profession of love, about how to respond to her. I had arranged to stay at a friend's house in Lafayette. It was a little over a two-hour drive from New Orleans depending on the traffic.

As I drove past Baton Rouge, the announcer stated that seven years earlier on October 25, 1984, Richard Brautigan, the writer, had been found dead in his California home. He was forty-nine years old at the time of his death, and the reporter stated that his death had been classified as a suicide.

As the sun hung high in its interstate picture frame in front of me, the memory chip in my head quickly recalled that Camus had said that the only true philosophical problem was that of suicide and whether to commit it. Camus, despite his stark existentialist underpinnings, had opined that suicide was not justified. Brautigan had apparently filed his dissenting opinion in 1984.

I could not recall all of the books by Brautigan which I had read. I did recall reading *In Watermelon Sugar* and *Confederate General at Big Sur*. I also recalled reading *The Hawkline Monster* and *Trout Fishing in America*.

While in law school, a psychology student I had been dating, Brandy, read *In Watermelon Sugar* at my recommendation. Brandy read it and thought it was "a very disturbing book." The more I thought about it, I recalled that in the short time we dated, she commented that she found many of my favorite books, including *The Catcher in the Rye* and *Still Life with a Woodpecker*, "disturbing." She was much more serious about our brief relationship than I was; more certain that I had a future which included her. I recalled, somewhat humorously, that what disturbed me most about Brandy was not her opinion of my favorite books. What disturbed me most about Brandy was that she gave terrible teeth dragging head.

The more I thought about it, the more vividly I recalled Brandy's comments about Brautigan. She had briefly ruined my pleasant and serene memories of *In Watermelon Sugar* by quizzing me constantly for a week or so on what IDEATH stood for in the book. She was convinced that IDEATH, which she pronounced I-death, was Brautigan's reference to the death of the individual soul in favor of a collectivized consciousness. "It's a very Eastern type of thing," I recall her saying on more than one occasion, to my gathering annoyance.

I was less than enthusiastic about her analysis for, although I viewed Brautigan's writings as marginally existentialist, I had never done much detailed philosophical analysis of Brautigan. I might spend hours debating about Camus or Shakespeare, but Brautigan was a glass of cheap wine to simply drink and enjoy. He was a writer who provided me an unusual respite and I resented too much analysis of his writings.

Brandy also quizzed me about why Inboil and his gang in *In Watermelon Sugar* cut off their noses. When I said that I had not given it much thought, she suggested it was an act of renouncing their physical bodies in favor of their spirituality.

"Why did they choose their noses to demonstrate this act of renunciation?" I recalled asking in a most serious tone, to chide her. "Perhaps they were only renouncing their olfactory senses," I said, in obvious jest. Brandy thought about my initial question and, pretending not to hear my remark about olfactory senses, then continued her questioning by asking me whether or not I thought Brautigan was a Marxist.

SIXTY-TWO

~

I could not distract myself for long with such distant memories. How to respond to Caroline? Here was a beautiful woman who possessed numerous qualities I admired. Thoughtful. Empathic. Intelligent and intellectual. Inquisitive. Sure, there was our disagreement over the existence of God, but so what. Why couldn't I feel something? I tried to bring some emotions forward, something beyond the everyday mundane and superficial need for companionship, but my intellect shut me down. I was used to sleeping around, used to the brief excitement of the physical conquest and its implied acceptance of me and used to an occasional woman who ignored my expressed intent and sought to put her claim on me. This was different and I lacked the capacity.

Then I had an idea. In hindsight it was a stupid idea. It was an intellectual solution to an emotional problem. But it rolled around in my head during the drive and gained slight purchase. She knew I never wanted to be married. So I thought to prove to her that she was special to me that I would propose, down on one knee, even buy a ring, the whole ritual, as soon as I returned home. But only on the condition that she not accept, that she turn me down. It was an intellectual's false sincerity. It was all I could come up with as a response. How shallow. How would she react to it?

SIXTY-THREE

~

I arrived in Lafayette and drove to my friend Paula's house
still thinking about my proposal. Paula was supposed to
be spending the weekend with her sister in Eunice, a
small town outside of Lafayette. She said that she would leave
her front door key in the mailbox. I had stayed with her on
occasion, when younger, in brief on again off again romantic
encounters. She understood my intent, that sex was currency,
and we remained friends long after the romantic ardor had
died. I was hoping to lay low at her house, read some books I
brought, and go out only to eat. However, when I pulled into
the driveway, Paula's car was still there and I could see the
front door of the house was open. Paula stepped out onto her
porch as I pulled further up the driveway. She stared at me.
She looked as if she was about to scold a child for their mis-
conduct during recess.

I had a brief sensation that there was something wrong. It
was a very personal premonition and a signal conveyed in what
appeared to be Paula's unnaturally slowed physical movements.
I was apprehensive as I got out of my car, but I could not have
explained why.

Paula waited on the porch for me to walk to her. She forced
a smile, a slight pensive smile, onto her face as I approached.

"Honey, Rebekah called," she said, as I got close. I had not
heard from Rebekah in a while and could not imagine how
she could have known I was headed to Paula's for the weekend.

Perhaps she had spoken to one of my friends. But whom? The premonition, like a blind man frantically seeking to escape from an unfamiliar room, returned to me again in the pause after Paula's statement. I stood directly in front of her. The blind man inside of me braced himself.

"I'm sorry to have to tell you this, but apparently your friend Caroline was involved in some type of serious accident."

My face must have lost some of its color. Paula moved reassuringly toward me. She placed her hands under my left arm and walked me two or three steps to a bench on the porch. She gently pressed down on my shoulders so that I would sit.

"What kind of accident? Is she all right?" As I asked, I knew that she was not. There was some karmic imbalance around me, that I was aware of on an instinctive level. Paula kneeled down and was eye level with me.

"All I know is that Rebekah said your friend Caroline died after being rushed to the emergency room of a hospital. She said to give you her love and call her if you need anything." I felt nothing for a moment. Then I cried uncontrollably, like a child. Like someone crying over the loss of an unconditional love. I lowered myself off of the bench onto the ground and fell hard into Paula's arms, placing my head on her shoulder. It couldn't be, I told myself. I continued to cry out loud, unencumbered by social etiquette. After several minutes I lifted my head up and looked at Paula through my tears. Her face showed genuine concern and fear. She had never seen me cry.

Paula said something about coming into the house and using the phone. I heard it, but I did not respond. I held Paula's hand as I stood up, breathed deep, and then without speaking, my voice had left me, I walked back to my car wiping tears from my face with the palms of my hands.

"You should wait awhile," Paula yelled to me. I then drove back to New Orleans, speaking out loud to Caroline, asking her for forgiveness, begging that it was not true, and pulling over to the side of the interstate on two occasions when my crying and my tears overtook me.

SIXTY-FOUR

~

There was a blue car in my driveway when I arrived at home. I did not recognize the car and there was no one in it. I got out of my car and grabbed my duffel bag with my books and clothes. I walked past the car in the driveway and pulled out my keys to open the front door. As I approached I heard someone in the house. I opened the door and I was startled to see a woman sitting on my sofa. She was crying. It was Loretta. We looked at each other. She was struggling to retain her composure. I noticed her mouth was open slightly and her lips were trembling.

"I didn't know where else to go," she said, her voice broken, while tears streamed down her face.

I dropped my duffel bag on the floor, closed the door and moved slowly, with familiarity, to sit next to her on the sofa.

"Caroline had mentioned that you always left a key in your mailbox, and . . . I hope you don't mind," she said, in a disjointed way, as she turned and looked at me. The fingers on her hands were locked together tightly in her lap. She was squeezing her hands together as if it would somehow help her control her emotions. She rocked back and forth ever so slightly, seeking to comfort herself, while seated on the sofa. Tears welled again in her eyes and then streamed down her cheeks.

I was observing her, but I felt like I was submerged under water. I had no ability to speak. When I opened my mouth, my vocal chords did not cooperate. My chest hurt. I had difficulty swallowing and had to try two or three times in order to swallow successfully.

Loretta leaned toward me and as she cried, she uneasily put her arms around my neck and embraced me, tentatively at first and then tightly. She rested her head on my shoulder and I felt her chest heave, as she struggled to breathe between tears. My chin rested on her left shoulder. I could feel myself shaking. I was cold. Loretta squeezed me with her arms. I saw my tears fall and then spread on the shoulder of the gray shirt she was wearing. I felt nauseated. I thought of Caroline. I thought of her telling me that she was in love with me. I had journeyed into darkness, the unfamiliar shadows of emotional pain had been loosened, and I fell into the belly of Jonah's whale. I passed out.

SIXTY-FIVE

~

When I awoke, I was laying awkwardly on the floor in my living room. Loretta had placed a sofa pillow underneath my head and was telling me to drink from a glass of water she held in her hand. She lifted my head up with one hand, motherly, and brought the glass to my mouth. I saw that Loretta's eyes were red, but she was not crying. I swallowed some water and she laid my head back on the pillow. I looked up at her. Silence passed between us. I may have slept for a while. I awoke certain that I had only dreamt Caroline had died.

"She died on her way to her parents' house in Austin," Loretta said, as she sat on the floor next to me. I maneuvered myself into a sitting position.

"What happened?" I was finally able to ask.

"She drove up to see her parents the other night and apparently she was hit by a drunk driver towing another vehicle. The towed vehicle, with no driver in it, hit her head on and forced her into a ditch on a two-lane highway near her parents' house. Her mother said the police said it was a hit and run. She was alive for several hours after the accident in a ditch on the side of the road and died later in the hospital."

"My God. When did it happen?" I mumbled.

"The best I could tell, it was around 11:00 p.m. yesterday. I called her mother this morning to make sure she arrived all right and she told me. After talking to her mother, I tried to reach you, but no one answered. Caroline had mentioned Rebekah's name to me. And before she left town she mentioned you were headed out as well to stay with your friend Paula. Turns out Rebekah and I have a mutual friend, so I got her number and called her to try to reach you."

My mind slowly played out, like a video screen, the sequence of events Loretta described. I saw Caroline's face clearly. I pictured her wearing a white cotton dress. Then I thought about our kiss after she told me she loved me. Was I the last person to ever kiss her? Was I the only person she was ever in love with?

Loretta and I sat on the floor for a while longer. I unloaded my thoughts telling Loretta about Caroline and our last conversation including her profession of love for me.

"Michael, she has been in love with you for a long time. We discussed it. She had to get over the issue of you not believing in God but it never deterred her. She was determined," Loretta said.

"I didn't know," I replied.

Then, as if we had been married for thirty years and were aware of each other's most intimate habits, Loretta and I began to prepare for a trip to Austin for the funeral. I grabbed a suit and tie and packed some clothes while Loretta called Caroline's mother.

I overheard Loretta speaking to the mother. She spoke in a very reassuring voice and told her we would be leaving shortly. She spoke to her in a tone of great familiarity.

Without discussion, we put my suit and duffle bag in Loretta's car. We drove to her house so she could pick up some clothes. I made reservations from her house for both of us at the Holiday Inn in Austin.

"Should we go to Caroline's house and pick anything up?" I asked, as I lifted Loretta's suitcase into her trunk. The thought of going through Caroline's belongings did not appeal to either one of us. It would have to be done eventually, but soon after I raised the issue, I knew that I was in no emotional condition to do such a thing. Loretta suggested waiting until we spoke with Caroline's mother. I nodded approvingly and then we got into the car.

SIXTY-SIX

~

We drove in a soul crushing reflective silence down I-10 and over the Mississippi River bridge in Baton Rouge, 60 miles away, before either of us spoke. Loretta indicated that she and Caroline had been meeting about once a week for coffee during the last month or so. Mostly, they just "gossiped," as she described it. Funny, but I could not, at that moment, imagine Caroline gossiping. I was also surprised that Caroline saw Loretta that often and I was unaware of it.

Loretta indicated more than once that she had never met anyone like Caroline. I noticed tears well in her eyes and fall down the arcs of her cheekbones as she spoke. Her voice trembled.

"She was so supportive of me, of my choices, of my history," she said. I mostly listened while Loretta spoke. The talking seemed to be doing her good. Intermittently, I would begin to feel light headed and nauseated. My world which I had constructed with its internal and external high walls was falling on top of me crumbling into ash. Although I couldn't see the future, I already knew, intuitively, that nothing would be the same. When my eyes welled up with tears, I would turn, look out the window and concentrate on the trees along the interstate. I wanted to be nothing more than a piece of that scenery. On more than one occasion I was momentarily convinced, by some defense mechanism, that Caroline's death was part of a dream from which I would awake at any time. I was completely

unprepared emotionally for her death. There were numerous
friends whose lifestyles were such that you accepted their death
before it ever happened. There was nothing in Caroline's life,
no flaw or imperfection, which gave any indication of an early
death.

As we drove and Loretta spoke, my mind raced back in
time and took count of the people whom I had known that
had died. It was the mental equivalent of a Westmoreland-style
body count.

At nine years of age, my five-year-old sister, Laura, and
her friend Maura, had died in a house fire while at play next
door with a Filipino playmate. I had only two recollections of
Laura, real or imagined I was unsure. The first was of her sing-
ing while we drove in a car. The second was of a moment at her
funeral when my uncle swore her body had not been burned,
but she had only suffocated.

At sixteen, my best friend Keith overdosed on acid. The
overdose didn't kill him, but it rendered him an eternal twelve-
year-old trapped in a 6'5" frame. He had played one year of
high school basketball, but quit because the coach ordered him
to cut his hair. I recalled that he had been institutionalized
in the state hospital in Mandeville for several years after his
overdose and on a weekend release, when I was in college, he
jumped from the Mississippi River Bridge to his death. I often
wondered if, just for a few moments, he realized his mental
state and decided to take his life.

At seventeen, a classmate named Rick died in a car accident
after a high school football game. I could not remember Rick's
face, but recalled he had black hair.

When I was twenty-seven, Stephanie committed suicide. We
never knew why. She was always sleeping with younger guys
and then getting drunk and telling sailor-type stories about

refractory periods and their sexual inabilities. I never did sleep with her.

When I was thirty, Sammy died of a brain aneurysm. He was sitting at his kitchen table with his wife, who he had met at one of my parties, complained of a headache and fell over dead. Sammy had survived Vietnam and law school. I vividly recalled him drunk and bored one night when we were in law school. On that night he advised some female college freshman that he was the "best pussy eater in the world." I recall the wolfish grin on his face after he made that declaration.

As my mind drifted away from these thoughts, I heard Loretta saying that Caroline's mother had said we could stay at her house instead of the hotel if we wanted.

SIXTY-SEVEN

~

e checked into the hotel and Loretta immediately called Caroline's mother. When she got off the phone, she told me that the funeral was scheduled for 1:00 p.m. the next afternoon at a local Methodist church. Loretta wanted to go visit with Caroline's mother. I told her to go without me. I didn't feel like I would handle such a visit very well. Loretta then left.

I changed clothes and walked outside and caught a cab. I recalled from previous visits to Austin that there was a place called The Hole in the Wall near campus where I could get something to eat. The cabby said very little during the drive.

When I arrived, I took a seat at the bar and ordered a sandwich and a beer. For the time being the suffocating weight of Caroline's death had disappeared. However, while I did not feel that pressure, I felt the fragmentation of it. My intellectual cage, the necessary armor that had protected me for so many years, that allowed me to live without needing anyone, had quickly fallen into pieces and with it, with that deconstruction, strange emotions were being loosened on me.

I finished my sandwich and switched from beer to gin. I began to feel like there was something I had meant to remember, a train of thought that had skipped the tracks, but I couldn't recall. My mind searched around in the dark for a word or phrase that would bring back what I was supposed to remember. I heard the radio in the background and suddenly

recalled that Caroline's death was on the same day, October
25th, that Brautigan's body was found. That's what I was trying
to remember. I wondered if that was supposed to be significant.

October 25. What was the significance of that date? In my
emotional state, I reached for an anchor of explanation. All
I could think of was that it was five days prior to my birthday and it was during the time period classified as Scorpio in
astrology. That was not very much information.

I thought about Brautigan and Caroline and wondered if
there were any parallels in their lives. I knew very little, if anything, about Brautigan other than the books of his which I had
read. I was fairly certain that it was he who was on the cover
of his books. But I wasn't sure.

I drank a few more drinks. It was close to 9:00 p.m.

"Where is the university's library?" I asked the bartender.
After rubbing his beard, as if this would produce the answer,
the bartender gave me directions.

I walked around for several minutes and after making a
few wrong turns, I found myself standing in front of the Perry
Castenada library. I immediately went inside, found the card
catalog, and looked under 'B' for Brautigan.

Mostly the library had books by Brautigan. I saw names of
books that I had not known Brautigan had written. There were
titles like, *June 30th, June 30th, The Tokyo-Montana Express, Sombrero
Fallout* and *So the Wind Won't Blow It All Away.* As I was looking
through the card catalog, an Orwellian big brother sounding
voice came over the intercom and announced, in the cloistered
silence, that the library would be closing in fifteen minutes.

I turned passed the books by Brautigan and found a book
by someone named Terence Malley on Brautigan and another
by Keith Abbott. Finally, there was an annotated bibliography
on Brautigan by a John F. Barber. I quickly jotted down the
Dewey-Decimal System numbers for these books on a piece of

scrap paper near the card catalogue. I stuffed the paper in my pocket and walked out of the library. I made my way back to Guadalupe Street and caught a cab to The Continental Club.

Years ago, I had gone to The Continental Club on the recommendation of a friend to see a young guitar player named Stevie Ray Vaughan. I still recall that there was only a $2.00 cover charge when we had gone to see him. Times had changed.

There was not much to the Continental Club. Everyone who was no-one was there. The atmosphere was similar to that of the Maple Leaf in New Orleans prior to the Maple Leaf charging a cover charge and marketing itself to attract tourists. I sat at the small bar and ordered a gin and tonic.

Before long, the bar filled up and a band called The Noble Savages began to play. Thankfully, the woman sitting next to me was willing to talk. After a brief introduction, I asked her if she had ever read any Richard Brautigan.

"I think I read *In Watermelon Sugar* and *So the Wind Won't Blow It All Away*," she stated loudly, so as to be heard over the band. I leaned toward her ear.

"What did you think?"

"*In Watermelon Sugar* was great, but *So the Wind Won't Blow It All Away* was his last novel and I think he was pretty fucked up by then."

"Do you know anything about how he died?" I asked, over the music. She indicated that she didn't know anything about it. She did, however, confirm, when I asked, that she thought that he was on the cover of his books.

SIXTY-EIGHT

~

Y ou are the only one who ever loved me without asking for anything in return," she said. Wet. I felt wet. I awoke suddenly as water hit me in the face. I had been dreaming. It was raining. I got to my feet quickly, slipped and fell down, got up and ran to the overhang in front of the library. My head hurt. I must have fallen asleep in front of the library. I looked down and noticed the grass stains on my jeans. I could not recall leaving The Continental Club, an apparent black out. Nevertheless, I had somehow managed to get back to the library. It was 8:00 a.m. I walked into the library as it opened. As I walked in the lobby of the library, I fished in my pockets until I found a crumpled piece of paper. I pulled it out and read the Dewey decimal numbers.

I found the section of the library that contained books about Brautigan and books by Brautigan. I found the annotated bibliography on Brautigan by John F. Barber. I sat down on the floor in the aisle and began to read the prologue. I quickly learned that in the early 80's, Brautigan taught creative writing at Montana State University. Barber had been one of his students.

The prologue was filled with a few other details about Brautigan's life. He had been divorced twice and had a daughter named Ianthe. He had never learned to drive and often stayed at the Alpine Motel on the outskirts of Bozeman, Montana. I recalled that I had stayed in Bozeman for a night in the summer of 1984 en-route to Glacier Park. He would have still been alive that summer. He also enjoyed drinking George Dickel. Barber indicated that he believed Brautigan could find no meaning in his life. He also felt Brautigan was upset that his later books received very little notoriety.

A second book on Brautigan by Terence Malley filled in a few additional facts. I learned that the woman at the bar was right, was Brautigan's last novel. Malley said that Brautigan's body was found in Bolinas, California. He died of a self-inflicted gunshot wound. He suggested Brautigan had probably planned the suicide for some time.

There was another book by Keith Abbott indicating Brautigan's wake was held on October 31, 1985 at Enrico's Café. There were more details about Brautigan's life. In 1977, Brautigan had married a Japanese woman named Akiko, whom he later divorced.

The author discussed Brautigan's childhood and noted that Brautigan never met the man he was named after, the man who was supposed to be his father. Brautigan had been abandoned by his mother at a hotel room when he was nine. In 1955, Brautigan was sent to the Oregon State Hospital and diagnosed as paranoid schizophrenic after having thrown a rock through a police station window.

As to In Watermelon Sugar, Abbott wrote that "Brautigan seems to be saying that in order for a utopian community to be successful, a great deal of emotional repression and deprivation is necessary." I thought of Brandy and then of Caroline. I put the book back on the shelf. Nothing seemed to connect. I found nothing in the books discussing whether Brautigan was religious. Still, as I sat on the floor in the aisle at the library, in my grief, in my search for some meaning to Caroline's death, I couldn't shake the feeling that there was a connection. That the similarity of the dates meant something.

I knew that I needed to get to the church for the funeral. Loretta had written the address down for me and I had it in my wallet. I left the library in a hurry so I could get back to the hotel, shower, and change.

SIXTY-NINE

～

I sat in the back of the church before the service began. Loretta tried unsuccessfully to get me to sit with her and Caroline's parents in the front pew. I noticed that there were only 20 or 30 people in the church. Most of those in attendance were older people whom I imagined were friends of Caroline's parents.

Caroline was dead.

Her mother turned in the pew and motioned for me to come to her. I got up involuntarily and with tears in my eyes walked to her. She stood up and reaching toward me squeezed my hands with hers, just like Caroline had done to me innumerable times. The gesture, part of our history, overwhelmed me. I fell into her small shoulder and wept. She held me close.

"I'm sorry," I heard myself say. Loretta stood up and steadied me. Caroline's mother looked at me peacefully as her husband sat stoically nearby.

"I want to tell you something," she said.

"Yes ma'am."

"Your given name is Michael Tusa right?"

"Yes ma'am."

"Well, I hope it is ok to tell you this." She paused.

"When the EMT's got to the accident site my dear Caroline was still alive. All those hours later." I bit down on my lip to try to stop the tears.

"I know one of those young men who is an EMT and was there. He goes to my church and I taught him in Sunday school. Anyway, he told me that as they were loading her up into the ambulance Caroline kept repeating a word that they did not understand. In fact, they didn't think it was a word."

"Yes Ma'am."

"From what they told me, and this is what I want you to know and carry with you, I think she was repeating your last name--Tusa--over and over again." I broke down again. Loretta wrapped her arms around me. "You were one of her last thoughts, and, perhaps, as her mind was searching for comfort in her pain she thought of you. I think it was a comfort to her to think of you. In fact, I'm sure of it," her mother said.

I could not stop crying. I wondered if Caroline was repeating my name wondering if I loved her. Loretta asked me to sit with them, but I declined and walked again to the back of the church after hugging Caroline's mother.

I faded in and out as the minister delivered a sermon on how Caroline had gone to be with her "true father." He droned on in a rehearsed pre-paid and monotone voice about how we should all rejoice at this fact even though we felt a personal loss in Caroline's death. "There is a greater love which we cannot understand," I heard him say.

At some point the minister indicated to the sparse crowd that if anyone wanted to say anything about Caroline, they could. I saw Loretta turn around to look at me. As she looked at me mournfully, but with encouragement, Caroline's mother turned to look at me also. She had a peaceful look on her face.

I thought to myself that I was too tangled in the knots of my emotions and too hung over to organize my thoughts. When Caroline's grandmother turned to look at me in the back of the church, several other people near the front of the church turned to see who, or what, she was looking at. The minister also looked in my direction. Caroline's mother waved for me to come to her.

I got up and my legs somehow carried me to her church pew. I leaned over toward her and past Loretta. She grabbed my hand, and looked deep into my eyes.

"Caroline spoke of you often to me. You were her nonbeliever friend whom she loved very much and I think she would have liked for you to say a few words." As I straightened up and let go of her hand, Caroline's mother continued to look at me. I tried hard to restrain the tears that welled up in my eyes.

As best I recall, I then walked up to the podium near the altar. Caroline's closed casket was a few feet away. I diverted my eyes away from the casket and looked down at the podium I now stood behind. There was a Bible at the podium and a microphone. I seem to recall that I stood for a few seconds before actually speaking.

What could I possibly say that could express my feelings toward Caroline; feelings the depth of which I did not realize existed and had immediately ambushed me in unimaginable ways, releasing my emotions, upon her death. I spoke as clearly as I could, occasionally pausing when tears took away my voice.

"I have been a friend of Caroline's for about four years. She was my best friend. It's true that sometimes you don't know what someone means to you until after they are gone. A missed opportunity. I am just beginning to understand and it will take me a while to sort it all out and put my own life back together, though I don't think the old pieces will fit together anymore. Caroline believed fervently in God. She and I spoke often about her religious beliefs and about my lack of religious beliefs. Caroline, my friend, in my experience, was a unique Christian. She was not afraid to think. She rejected the Christianity of most self-professed Christians, what St Thomas, the Catholic saint, called cultivated ignorance. She could think about the inconsistencies in her belief system without fear because she did not believe in a brick building called a church, or a man called a priest, but rather in something more personal; in a God that was larger than the religious practices of this church; in a God that focused solely on how we treat one another. Caroline was proof that thinking does not kill religious spirit. Indeed, her life proved it can enrich it. Her life was proof that reason and religious belief are not incompatible. And for me, having lost her friendship, having lost her unconditional love, it's hard to say....She broke through my darkness with a message of love....I heard you Caroline....I heard you when you told me to trust others. I heard you when you told me I could love and that I deserved to be loved....I heard you when you told me I had worth....I promise to drop my guard more often, to learn how to feel even if it leads me to be hurt, to let people in, and I promise to try to live in a way that does not disappoint you."

At that point, I now recall that the minister approached me and put his hand on my shoulder. I turned to look at him. He appeared to be in his mid to late 50's. He looked well fed. I recall hostility rising inside of me.

"Son, that's enough," he said sternly. Loretta told me that she had started walking towards me as I pushed his hand away from me forcefully and stared at him. She told me that with tears running down my face I then turned and walked away from the podium, down to the casket, placed my hands on it, told Caroline's mother and father good bye and then walked out of the church in silence.

SEVENTY

~

I could not count the number of times over the next month I awoke in the morning, or in the middle of the night, still believing in those first few seconds of semi-consciousness between the dusk and dawn of reason, that her death was a dream. I awoke fully each time to the painful realization that it had actually occurred. Caroline was dead and, I was beginning to understand, how her death changed me. It opened a closed door to my emotions, to my need for others, and left me with a debt to her I could not begin to repay. But initially I simply felt lost and in that condition of loss I became common and grasped for simple certitude. I felt like a man in a boat in the middle of the ocean with no stars above, no navigational instruments and no way to be assured of the proper direction, abandoned to the Homeric fates.

One day, not long after the funeral, perhaps depressed, as I was getting out of my car in the driveway at the house, after going through the motions of work, and the new law practice I had set up with Singleton, a yellow and green bug of some type abruptly landed on my car antenna. I had never seen this particular type of bug before. I closed the car door and the bug flew from the antenna and landed on the railing near the front porch of the house. As I walked toward the front door, the bug flew hard into the front door three or four times in a row as if trying to get inside the house. The bug then landed on the front door doorknob.

I was perfectly sober. Yet, I was convinced in an instant that the bug was Caroline, or a message from her. I leaned my back against the front porch railing. I watched the bug for 20 or 30 seconds. At that moment, the whole world was reduced to me and the bug. It did not move. I began to talk to it as if it was Caroline. I told myself that if it stayed on the doorknob for another 10 seconds that was proof. I said my thoughts out loud for the bug to hear. The bug remained perfectly still on the doorknob. It slowly moved its wings, as if it was trying to decide whether to fly away. It was comforting to me to have spoken. I fell quiet and tried to clear my mind. Within a minute the bug flew from the door knob. I followed it into the yard before it flew away out of sight.

I spent more time in the library, in the following weeks, researching on Brautigan and trying to determine if there was a link between his death and Caroline's. I hit a dead end when I confirmed that Brautigan's body was found on October 25, but that he had probably committed suicide a week or so earlier. There appeared to be no connection as to the date.

SEVENTY-ONE

~

It was 1:00 a.m. and I lay in bed briefly awake. Alone in the darkness of my room, unable to sleep, I tried to bring forward in my mind Caroline's image of God but I couldn't. The images ingrained in me were from cheap religious paintings. I saw painted pictures of Christ from my childhood—portrayed as a young white man with long well groomed hair and beard and his hands extended from his sides, or with a crown of thorns on his head looking skyward. Blood drops trickled from the thorns down his temple into his neatly trimmed beard. His face bore the artist's expression of one contemplating another world, desirous of leaving this one.

The weight of Caroline's death crushed any lingering inhibitions from my Catholic childhood to confront that image of God, or the son of God. With my best friend's death, the few rules of religious etiquette that may have remained with me were dismantled, ground into dust and blown away by the dark wind of my pain. I confronted that image in my mind not as a servant, not as one seeking counsel, but as an equal. I feared no ramification for my impertinence. I feared no physical pain or damnation. And like Job I spoke to this image. "Why?"

I listened intensely in the quiet of my room. I sharpened my senses and tried to focus my eyes in the dark. I waited for some Jobian response, as I issued repeated challenges to this hiding deity, some sign from Him acknowledging my confrontation. None was forthcoming. This was not a God that spoke to me.

I suddenly found that I recalled from my youth some of the rituals of Catholicism. I remembered 104 candles in black wrought iron stands of red glass which were to be lit in order to help a soul stranded in purgatory: A 104 bus tickets to heaven for Uncle Joe.

I recalled the ringing of a bell by an altar boy, in a black and white robe, as the priest lifted the host with both hands from the altar. My inner ear echoed with: "And He took the bread, broke it and gave it to them saying, take this bread for it is my body."

I recalled dimly early morning stations of the cross and monthly trips to the black screened confessionals at the rear of the church. "Bless me Father, for I have sinned," I heard myself say.

I fell back into a dream state unsure of whether I was awake or asleep. The gloaming of sleep had overtaken me, but it was not yet full night. I dreamt fitfully. The painted pictures of the mystery of Christ disappeared before me and an image of a God very different from the pictures of my Catholic youth slowly appeared in my dream state. I saw this God seated in a large high back white chair at a desk working alone in a sterile and silent white walled laboratory. He had a dark Mediterranean complexion and was bald on the top of his head with white and gray wisps of untrimmed curls hanging to the collar of a thin layered white robe, which he wore. He had an un-groomed black and white beard, large unkempt eyebrows and soft, but lifeless, black eyes set deep in his face. His forehead was covered with wrinkles. He was old and looked very tired. The type of tiredness that comes from a long struggle, from carrying an overwhelming burden, like the lingering illness of a loved one. He appeared to be very heavy and was broad but stooped shouldered from advanced age.

I entered the laboratory through an open doorway. It was difficult for me to move forward, to move my body, it was as if I my entire body was partially paralyzed and the invisible Newtonian ether slowed me. He did not acknowledge my presence, but continued to focus, undisturbed, on an unusually large worn leather ledger in front of him on his desk. The ledger was open and equally oversized pages were on each side. I looked for angels and saw none. I listened for comforting harps and there were none.

His hands were massive and calloused like those of someone arthritic, who had spent his entire life in manual labor. He placed one of those hands on the open page of the ledger and leaning forward, as if to bring the page into focus to weary eyes, moved his stubby index finger in a straight line across the middle of the page. His motions were very slow as those of the elderly who are losing their combat with physical deterioration.

I struggled to step forward a few feet. I tried to speak, but found I had no voice. I felt myself choke. He did not look at me. He did not speak to me, or acknowledge my presence. He turned in his chair slowly. He then lifted his great mass unsteadily and, after a pause, shuffled barefoot and silently toward a glass door on the other side of the room. The door was crooked, a loose hinge perhaps. He stopped near the door, breathed heavily, before moving on, and then, in a shuffling gait, disappeared.

I tried to follow, but could not move forward. I was eight or ten feet from the desk. I looked around the room and noticed it was otherwise unremarkable in description. The lines of the walls in the room began to fade away in my dream. It was as if a Hollywood movie set was slowly disappearing. I looked quickly at the ledger which lay open on the desk. I could see the pages to which it was open, the page he had set his hand on. My eyes focused on the page as the surroundings of the room continued to fade away. The page was white, unlined and blank.

I awoke with full memory of the dream, all of its aspects. I thought of the caution in the Talmud that "a dream is its own interpretation." If so what did this dream mean?

SEVENTY-TWO

~

I was not suicidal, but had the strangest feeling, daily, for several months, that Caroline was pulling me to
her, wanting me to accompany her on her new journey,
wishing me to abandon this life and follow her. She repeatedly appeared in my dreams. It was confusing and frustrating.

As I went through the motions of practicing law, I felt it
emotionally and physically. I drank in nightly excess after work
hours and didn't care. I drove at excessive speeds in my car, unafraid. One dark and rainy night on a wet highway I went into
a curve too fast and my car spun out in a complete 360 degrees.
When the car jolted to a stop my heart was not even beating
fast. I was detached from my life, the horrors and the fears, my
emotions looking for moorings that I had never built, while
waiting for what she would do with me, hopeful and confused
at the same time.

And then one morning I recall well, after the many that
had run together in emotional struggle, I woke up feeling
different, lighter. Something had changed that was not of my
doing. I walked into the bathroom and looked at myself in the
mirror, hollow eyed, and I even looked different. I looked again
hard at myself and said these words out loud: "She let me go."

SEVENTY-THREE

~

I'm still having problems with the unfairness of this," I said.
It had been six months since Caroline's death.
"Which aspect?" Loretta asked, seated as usual in her leather chair with a notepad in her lap. She looked over the top of her glasses at me, calmly, and waited for a reply. I knew that I had interrupted her day by simply showing up to see if she was in. I had often done that, since she had opened her office, during the past six months. We had talked about the loose ends in my life: the childhood I would never recall, and the deadening of my emotions which awoke with Caroline's death.

"It's hard to imagine that someone could believe so fervently in a God and there not be one for that person," I said, adjusting myself on the sofa her clients used for counseling sessions. I knew that part of me, that part I had in the past classified in others as exhibiting frailty, wanted to believe there was a God for Caroline. "She structured her whole life around her belief in God, her entire value system," I continued.

"Michael, everyone structures their life around something. It can be an idea, a deity, a profession, a relationship," she replied, leaning back in her chair.

"It just doesn't seem like something," I mumbled.

"To what extent have you structured your life around your belief that there is no God?" she asked. "We have had numerous discussions where you indicated that because you did not believe in God you had to create your own value system and, in a sense, become your own God. Isn't that system then based on your atheism?"

I followed her logic to a certain point. However, my mind detected a difference between my believing in nothing and Caroline believing in something. If I died, nothing, it seemed to me, would be lost. Because she believed in something that I didn't think existed, her death seemed more tragic. I tried to relay these thoughts to her.

"First, believing in God and not believing in God are both belief systems. I learned that from you," she said. "In fact, as you said to me long ago, it is probably easier to believe in God than not to believe in God."

I recalled as she spoke that I had often felt, too simplistically, that believing in a certain religion only required one decision, and that was to believe. After that, the religious dogma determined all other decisions for the individual. In contrast, a nonbeliever had to make each decision as it arose. The rationale, in light of Caroline's death, and the way in which she had believed, now seemed distant to me.

"In the final analysis, there really is very little difference between the thinking believer like Caroline and a thinking atheist like yourself. I think Caroline came to realize that," she said. "Look, I was reading a book called *Doubt, A History* and... here it is," she said picking up a piece of loose leaf paper. "I wrote this down for you. The author writes: 'Great believers and great doubters seem like opposites, but they are more similar to each other than to the mass of relatively disinterested or acquiescent men and women.'"

"I'm not sure I believe that anymore. At least as it relates to Caroline and me," I replied.

"Why not?"

"She was a real Christian, not the cheap grace kind. And I'm not sure what I am," I said.

"What is a real Christian?" Loretta asked, with obvious interest. I paused to collect my thoughts before answering.

"I would say someone who is non-judgmental of others. Someone who can love all people unconditionally, who doesn't fight, criticize, or throw the first punch, and who puts serving others above their own self-interest."

"That would be pretty rare. A Bodhisattva," Loretta opined.

"She was that," I said.

The lessons of Caroline's death, if there are lessons in the death of another, even a year out, were growing and coming more sharply into focus for me. Her death had shattered whatever perception I had that I could spend my life without emotion, living on my self-created island and needing no one. For the year since her death I had to struggle with my biggest nemesis, my emotions. I had learned to intellectualize my whole life as a defense to my emotions and the vulnerability those emotions could cause me. My intellect, in a very real sense, had kept my emotions caged. Her death had turned the key to that cage in a way that no other loss in my life was ever capable and now the cage was open. I was often ill-equipped to deal with the emotions that escaped from the cage. I was learning that my emotions, even as ill-formed as they were, were far more formidable when loosened than my intellect's ability to restrain them. And because of Caroline I began to give my emotions free rein, opened my hand, and exposed myself to the world, to the pain, and sometimes just let things happen. It was awkward. Small steps, often stumbling, but I was trying my best to honor her.

And love? I wasn't sure I would ever be capable of it, but she had shown me what unconditional love looked like, the warmth of its embrace, and I would never be the same as a result. It had an indelible effect on me, a remembrance for a lifetime, that cancelled out and superseded other rejections.

But most of all, the year since her death had made me realize that Caroline had, during the time of our friendship, become an invaluable reference point for me. She was, ironically, my reference point in a world with no God. Without her, like I did after leaving home at 17 years of age, I was having to learn to navigate through my life again.

I repeated softly, but out loud, a few lines from *The Little Prince*:

> *But if you tame me, then we shall need each other. To me you will be unique in all the world. To you, I shall be unique in all the world...*

That's as much as you can ask from any relationship I thought. It's the fact that you tamed me when I wasn't even aware of it, I said to my mental image of Caroline.

Loretta looked at me with her hands folded over her notepad.

"Do you ever have days where you feel you have come to terms with Caroline's death?" she then asked. I had thought about this many times, used my intellect to try to resolve it.

"The only time Caroline's death fits, or is not unsettling to me, is when I recall her beliefs and then force myself not to think any further about the logic of those beliefs." Loretta looked at me, a bit puzzled.

"I know it sounds odd," I said, looking down at the floor. "But what I do is to simply allow myself to believe that there is a God for Caroline solely because she believed in one and her belief was a beautiful thing to behold."

"And what about for you?" Loretta asked.

"I don't matter," I replied. Loretta fell silent, as if considering my proposition.

"So there is a God for those who believe?" she asked.

"I am answering your question of whether I have come to terms with Caroline's death," I replied, somewhat analytically. "And it's only when I create a belief that there is a God only for Caroline because she believed and then not think about the illogic of that belief any further that her death is not unsettling." I paused realizing that Loretta was not completely understanding what I was saying. "In other words, I'm not proposing a grand theory about the existence of God," I said. "Just that there was a God for Caroline. There must be. There has to be," I said, emphatically. Loretta leaned back in her chair and looked at me supportively, as if she understood something deeper.

"That's called faith, Michael."

Yet, as I thought about my rationalization of there being a God for Caroline simply because she believed in one, I once again had that feeling of a weight being lifted from my body. It was hard to describe. Some ethereal chemical had loosened in my brain and I felt a lightness of being that was otherwise unfamiliar to me.

"Do you want to continue talking?" Loretta asked. I shook my head negatively.

"No, thanks."

SEVENTY-FOUR

~

I waved off Emily the bartender when she asked if I wanted a second gin and tonic. It was late on a damp and crowded Saturday night at the Maple Leaf. I had not been drinking much lately, didn't feel the need to do so, and had not seen anyone I knew in the hour I had been seated at the bar. I had resolved to leave and head home in the next few minutes to get some sleep.

The Cajun band File' was playing that night. I turned slightly on the barstool so that I could see the dance floor. The band began to play a Cajun two-step. I watched the ten or so couples on the dance floor and their different styles. I had not paid that close attention to dancing styles in a few years. I thought of Caroline dancing and the years I spent watching her and our secret of what it meant to her. I wished I had a picture of the two of us dancing. My memory would have to suffice. Still, years of watching made it clear that most of the dancers had some unique style which they brought to the dance. It could be in how they led their partner, or how they followed the lead, or as simple as the lowering of a shoulder and leaning slightly, affectionately, into their partner. But it only worked if the two dancers worked in harmony and not against each other.

I noticed a college-age girl in a flowered yellow dress. She was dancing with a thin black man, probably in his 50's, wearing a black cowboy hat. As he spun her around, I saw that most of his front teeth were missing. The only tooth I could see as he grinned was gold.

The young girl's blonde hair covered her face as she twirled. For that brief moment I saw Caroline in her movements. The repetition in the movements seemed significant. I knew Caroline was dead. I knew now that it was not a dream, but for the space of those movements something of her was here and now. Repetition, I thought, is more than coincidence. Like when Caroline's mother squeezed my hand, it was Caroline's squeeze. The pebble drops, one life ends, but the ripples continue to move across the surface of time. Maybe, just maybe I thought, it moves in both directions.

The young girl's hair fell back in place by her neck, I saw her face. Her mouth was opened and she was smiling widely. It almost appeared as if she was laughing. She must have sensed I was looking at her. She looked at me and her face was calm. I smiled back at her. And as I smiled I realized slowly that I did believe in something I couldn't prove. Not in a God, not in a job, or in my intellect, but in a friendship, in a relationship with another human being.

EPILOGUE

~

Seven months after Caroline's death I was sitting in a restaurant alone after work. I had cut off all my hair and was wearing a suit and tie. A woman I did not know approached my table and said that a photographer friend of hers had taken a picture of me and a woman dancing at the New Orleans Jazz and Heritage Festival a year earlier for a photo contest. How this woman could have recognized me I have no idea. I asked if she could get her friend to send me the photo and I gave her my mailing address. This photo of Caroline and I dancing arrived several days later with no postmark and no return address on the manila envelope.

Caroline had often appeared to me in my dreams for years after her death, especially when times were stressful. It was always a comfort. In early 2000 I had a very hectic schedule with trials, running my law practice and the vicissitudes of a new marriage. But at that point in time Caroline was no longer showing up in my dreams. She and I had often discussed the Buddhist notion that there were 32 levels of existence and she wondered if one could communicate from one level to another level or if anything changed as you moved up the levels. It was a topic we discussed a few times. So with her no longer appearing in my dreams and with me being worn out, one day, sitting at my office desk, I said to her image: "Maybe you can't show up in my dreams anymore because you moved to a new level, but just let me know you are ok any way that you can." About 10 minutes later the phone in my office rang. It was a law school classmate, Peggy, who had known Caroline and who lived in Alexandria, Louisiana. I had not heard from Peggy in years. She wanted me to know that she had been at a meeting of Christian women in north Louisiana and met an older woman who turned out to be Caroline's mother. Ms. Gandy, Caroline's mother, upon learning who Peggy was had immediately asked her "How is Tusa?" and then asked Peggy if she could connect us. Needless to say I was shaking when I got off the phone. I calmed myself and called Ms. Gandy. I learned that her husband, Caroline's father, had recently died. She and I kept in touch over the next year or so and then one day she called and told me that her youngest daughter, Robin, who I had never met, and Robin's husband, Brendan, were moving from New York to the New Orleans area and asked if I could look in on them once they got settled. This I did and shortly thereafter Robin became pregnant. It was a difficult pregnancy and about 5 months into it Brendan had to move back to New York for work. The babies were born, twins, and along with

Robin lived with me and my then wife, Karen, for the first few months of their lives. The twins are named Caroline (called Rosie) and Madeline. I was asked by Robin and Brendan to be their godfather and I accepted.

Ultimately Caroline's mother moved down to live with Robin and her family and we spent many hours together in discussion. She would often squeeze my hands like Caroline did to show her affection for me. She passed away a few years ago but I got to know her well. The twins are growing up and remain a big part of my life.